"The Matthews have a unique way of get.........................hile
also helping them identify practical step..................... life
outcomes of their desires. Rarely do I find a business ....own,
but *The Human Cloud* is one of those rare finds."

—Betsy Westhafer,
CEO of The Congruity Group,
Author, Speaker, and Podcaster

"*The Human Cloud* is a must-read book to assist you, your organization, and your team in using the power of artificial intelligence to augment workplace capabilities. AI will not replace workers but enable them to work smarter!"

—Jeanne Meister,
Founding Partner of Future Workplace and Coauthor of
*The Future Workplace Experience: 10 Rules For Mastering
Disruption in Recruiting and Engaging Employees*

"The Matthews provide an explicit playbook to tap into the magic of the freelance economy; *The Human Cloud* will benefit the world's most talented individuals for years to come."

—Michael Burdick,
CEO of Paro

"In order to understand why and how to come out on top, read this book!"

—Michael Solomon,
Coauthor of *Game Changer* and Cofounder of 10x Management,
10x Ascend, Brick Wall Management, and Musicians On Call

"*The Human Cloud* is the critical guide to our times . . . the best first step any leader can take to build the future that puts people first and creates the future of work."

—Stephanie Nadi Olson,
Founder of We Are Rosie

"Whether you are a freelancer, want to become one, work with one, or have never heard of one, you will be able to feel inspired by this work."

—Laurel Farrer,
Founder and CEO of Distribute Consulting
and Former COO of Yonder

"Freelancing is inevitably completely different from what you think it's going to be like when you first plan your escape from corporate 9–5. *The Human Cloud* takes you into the stories and experiences of people just like you and me."

—Petra Manos,
CEO of The Quantified Web and
Podcast Panelist at *The Freelancer Show*

"Refreshing, yet realistic. The Matthews provide a clear roadmap for where we're going and what we need to do to get there."

—Katherine Brune,
Owner and Principal consultant of WorkSprout LLC and
Former Employee Well-Being & Benefits Director at SunTrust

"Before the disruptive storm of the human and machine cloud-building on the horizon surprises you when it is too late, read the Matthews' book now to prepare yourself to thrive in this new economy."

—Larry English,
President of Centric Consulting and Author of
Office Optional: How to Build a Connected Culture with Virtual Teams

"*The Human Cloud* lays out the case for using data analytics and AI to make remote workers more efficient while delivering higher quality—this is the next leap forward in making digital workers happier and more productive."

—Chris Keene,
CEO of Gigster

"A must-read for anyone looking for more meaning, purpose, and control over their work, and for leaders who want to employ and use talent in groundbreaking ways."

—Keith Rollag,
Dean of F. W. Olin Graduate School of Business, Babson College

"The authors show us how both automation and freelance models converge to create new and increased opportunity for every one of us. A highly readable book that makes complex challenges clear, simple, and tangible."

—Michael R. Solomon, PhD,
Professor of Marketing, Saint Joseph's University

"Packed with useful tips and information, *The Human Cloud* will not only help you to explore and understand how the entire employment landscape is changing but also how to best prepare, position, and market yourself for the future."

—Russ Crowley,
Microsoft Word Consultant, www.russcrowley.com

THE HUMAN CLOUD

HOW TODAY'S CHANGEMAKERS USE ARTIFICIAL INTELLIGENCE AND THE FREELANCE ECONOMY TO TRANSFORM WORK

MATTHEW MOTTOLA
AND MATTHEW COATNEY

HarperCollins
LEADERSHIP

AN IMPRINT OF HARPERCOLLINS

To you, Grandma, for teaching me how to smile, missing your smile every day.

—*Matthew Mottola*

To my wife, Jenn, for always supporting my various pipe dreams, and to my children, Parker, Chase, and Lacey, who will inherit this new world of work.

—*Matthew Coatney*

Published by HarperCollins Leadership, an imprint of HarperCollins Focus LLC.

Any internet addresses, phone numbers, or company or product information printed in this book are offered as a resource and are not intended in any way to be or to imply an endorsement by HarperCollins Leadership, nor does HarperCollins Leadership vouch for the existence, content, or services of these sites, phone numbers, companies, or products beyond the life of this book.

ISBN 978-1-4002-1974-2 (eBook)

ISBN 978-1-4002-1973-5 (HC)

Library of Congress Control Number: 2020947367

CONTENTS

Introduction   ix

GOODBYE, "OLD" WORLD!   1

1 The Office Is Broken   3

2 Rise of the Changemaker   13

THE HUMAN CLOUD   29

3 Rise of the Human Cloud   31

4 Why Changemakers Are Moving to the Human Cloud   41

5 How Changemakers Are Thriving in the Human Cloud   57

6 Why Tapping into the Human Cloud Is the New Corner Office   69

7 How to Tap into the Human Cloud   80

8 Why Organizations Embrace the Human Cloud   92

9 How Organizations Embrace the Human Cloud   100

10 What's on the Horizon for the Human Cloud   107

THE MACHINE CLOUD   115

11 Rise of the Machine Cloud   117

12 How to Work in the Machine Cloud   126

13 Tapping into the Machine Cloud   136

CONTENTS

14 Unlocking the Machine Cloud in Organizations   151

15 What's on the Horizon   158

HELLO, "NEW" WORLD!   167

16 Release the Changemaker   169

Acknowledgments   179

Index   185

About the Authors   193

INTRODUCTION
THE FUTURE IS *YOU*

The 2015 Spanish animated short *Alike* follows a father and son as they live their lives at work and school. Both characters start out colorful, but as they are forced to sit through the monotonous drudgery of their stifling routines, they begin to drain to a pale white. Their spirit and energy fade, and as the story progresses, their loving relationship fades as well.

Much like a Pixar short, in eight minutes this film captures a universal truth in a gut-wrenching, tear-jerking way: traditional corporate work is both figuratively and literally killing us.

Meanwhile, another world has changed our lives and the lives of those you'll meet in this book. Consider it our generation's Gold Rush. Instead of gold, we have opportunity. Instead of shovels, we have what we call the *human cloud* (the virtual talent workforce) and the *machine cloud* (intelligent automation). And instead of miners, we have you—the changemaker—to reject the status quo and change the world.

Unfortunately, not all change is positive. As product leaders on the front lines, we've witnessed this transformation firsthand. While the headlines are catchy—the robots are coming, we'll all be free agents in the gig economy—what we're actually building and the change we're creating can be terrifying. Think George Orwell or Ayn Rand. While highly paid radiologists are being replaced by software that can detect cancer in MRI scans better than a human, global talent marketplaces are replacing careers and salaries with unstable, hourly incomes and no benefits or paid time off.

But it doesn't have to be this way! Yes, there will be a Herculean slash to the way we've worked for the past 150 years. Yes, if you're sitting in a corner office, holding onto that paper diploma for dear life, or want the life your parents had, this should scare the crap out of you. But no, this isn't doomsday. It's a new day, with a new path to opportunity and a new model of work that can replace corporate tyranny with autonomy, flexibility, and control.

Some of you already work this way. Others want to work this way. No matter where in the journey you are, this book will show you what's possible with this radically redistributed opportunity.

ABOUT YOU

You're a changemaker. You strive to find meaning through your work and love what you do. You don't kiss ass. You don't punch in, then punch out. And you'll trade the corner office for moving the world forward any day.

Unfortunately, today's model of work wasn't built for you. It was built for your output and obedience, but not your high-flying ideas or innovation. Until now.

Yesterday, our path was well defined: go to a good school, get a good job, and give up your freedom to the boss and the company until, well, you become the boss.

Today, our path is largely undefined, in a good way. It's about accumulating valuable experiences and producing amazing outcomes, but in a nonlinear way. To the outside eye, it may look bold, chaotic, and—depending on the audience—downright irresponsible. Going this route gets you a lot of "Isn't it time to settle down?" or "Get a real job" comments. But to the insider's eye, the most successful and enduring path is becoming a changemaker, shaping the world around us. Your age, industry, or location doesn't matter. A forty-five-year-old healthcare worker in Cincinnati is just as capable as a twenty-six-year-old software developer in Silicon Valley (seriously).

A GLIMPSE OF THIS WORLD

The reward for becoming a changemaker is choice and opportunity.

Today's changemakers have the *choice* to work where they want. With whom they want. And on what they want. Take J Cheema, a designer based in Portland, Oregon, who left a lucrative role at Nike to work through the human cloud platform Upwork. (Yes, his first name is J—how awesome is that?)

The scope and scale of J's work hasn't changed. He works with brands like Exxon-Mobil, YouTube, GE, and Adidas. But in his words, "I decide on my clients and projects and choose when and where to work. I'm in complete control of my day."

Changemakers also have a personalized path to *opportunity*. There's no "set path"—rather there's a world of possibilities built around their unique situations. Take Gordon Shotwell, who was on a traditional path to becoming a lawyer but decided he wanted something different. Instead of going back to school, he taught himself how to work with the machine cloud and used projects in the human cloud to apply what he learned. He ultimately landed a full-time role doing what he loves, helping people understand artificial intelligence.

Changemakers help more than just themselves. They're fundamentally rewiring how organizations operate and serve their customers. Take the digital experience now possible for customers of a beloved motorcycle manufacturer headquartered in the Midwest. Riders wanted to connect with each other and the road, beyond paper maps and leather chaps. But let's face it—top tech talent is hard to find, especially if you're not a large tech company on the coast. Thanks to changemaker Brandon Bright, this organization harnessed the human cloud to design, develop, and support a mobile app that has over 150,000 downloads and a 5-star rating (with over 8,000 reviews).

The reason this is possible is because the new tools of the changemaker are the human and machine clouds. The human cloud is the new work platform, a project-based world where collaborators meet and work together outside of traditional full-time roles. And the machine cloud is the use of advanced technology to handle the "simple but time-consuming stuff" that gets in the way of delivering our unique value to the world.

Don't worry, you're not too late. The party is just starting, and there's enough opportunity for everyone. But the sooner you begin, the greater return you'll have. So, let's get started.

WHAT YOU CAN EXPECT

Expect to get a good taste of what's out there along with actionable steps to be effective in this new world. And sure, we'll sprinkle in some dad jokes for good measure.

This book has about 20 percent of the knowledge you can get through books, reports, presentations, and the like. As product nerds, we don't live and die by how much we know, but rather by what we can ignore. Instead of reciting every statistic (there are lots), we focus on essentials you can start using today.

Like all products, this book comes with warnings and disclaimers.

First, by the time you read this, parts will already be outdated. Sorry, that's the new norm of accelerated change. But even though some information may be out-of-date, and products may have come and gone just in the time it took from draft to published book, we strove to focus on what's true today that will still be true in the next ten or twenty years. While the only thing faster than swipes on Tinder are technology life cycles these days, the principles in this book are time-tested and will be safe for future generations.

Second, this book will not make you rich. Sorry. But it will provide you with an objective guide to build your foundation and tap into virtual work and automation. It's up to you to work your ass off, personalize these principles to your unique situation, and create a little luck.

We cannot stress this enough. There are no get-rich-quick schemes. People may make things look simple, but underneath the surface is a ton of blood and sweat to do anything meaningful. It's the iceberg analogy—you only see a sliver of the hard work that is underneath the surface. Be prepared to work hard, and know that it's all about incremental improvements and continual growth. That's the real key to enduring success.

THE FUTURE IS HUMAN

One last thing to keep in mind as you read the book. As the world gets more "gig-based" and automated, it will exponentially increase the importance of being uniquely human. Robots are boring. Humans are not. As you embrace your changemaker journey, we challenge you to be as human as possible. If you need a little nudge, start with a fun fact . . . let us embarrass ourselves first.

Matt M: I was unknowingly filmed in a Chinese Viagra promo. Somewhere in China, expect to see me with a thumbs-up behind the words *erectile dysfunction*.

Matt C: I was a punker in high school (admittedly I was a big teddy bear underneath the black trench coat and skull rings). At different times I had blue, green, and blond hair. Take that, corporate America.

We can't wait to show you this new world of work! As you can probably tell, this book is very personal to us, so expect some emotional baggage.

All right, let's roll!

Sincerely,

The Matthews

GOODBYE, "OLD" WORLD!

THE OFFICE IS BROKEN

IT'S NOT JUST YOU, THE TRADITIONAL
CORPORATE WORKPLACE IS UNRAVELING

Dear Changemaker,

We appreciate your drive and enthusiasm to make the world a better place. It's endearing. But we really don't care. We'd rather treat you like a cog. Force you to follow our "best practices." Drain you out of opportunity. And if you're obedient enough, we will reward you with some peanuts and a corner office where you can look down on those not as obedient as you. We know you came here to change the world. But we don't want change. In fact, we really don't want you. We just want your output—and to keep your skill set away from our competitors. So, here's your seat. Here's some Kool-Aid. We apologize in advance for when we lay you off. Thank you for your service.

Sincerely,

Your Future Employer

I never formally received the above letter. But many of us accepted the above social contract the moment we started working.

I learned this the hard way in my first real job. I wrote an article that gained global recognition and used it as a springboard to launch an offering that hit over $100,000 of revenue within the first two weeks. Being young and naive, I expected that the person who built it would be the one who owned it. But instead of leadership embracing my contribution, I was told it could only be 10 percent of my time, while they brought in an "experienced" person to lead it.

Then came my second real job. Same start—prove my stripes, drive a project to a point of tangible business value. This time I didn't get sidelined. Instead, the credit went to someone at the top.

I wanted to believe both experiences were flukes. Or that it was a me thing. But the more I heard from changemakers like you, the more my stories seemed calm by comparison. And the more the reality of being a changemaker within the traditional office became clear: The office wasn't built for us. It was built for obedient cogs willing to trade their autonomy, creativity, and at times morality for the company.

Peter Hinsenn of nexxworks describes our disconnect perfectly: We "are Elon Musks . . . in a Jack Welch (GE) company." Laurence Van Elegem of nexxworks says of changemakers, "It's just as difficult to keep them as it is to find them. Not just because the competition is always trying to lure them away, but because there is often a disconnect between these innovator profiles and the company DNA."

It's fun to generalize. All organizations are evil. All people in power are insecure tyrants. Obviously, this isn't entirely true. Organizations can be beautiful things. They can foster growth, accelerate learning, and provide serious meaning and belonging. And for every uplifting organization, there are countless mentors and role models holding power yet making everyone around them better. Take Bill Campbell, former CEO of Intuit and coach of Silicon Valley's greatest due to his servant leadership. Bill's leadership mindset was, "Think that everyone who works for you is like your kids."

On the flip side, the new world of work is not a panacea. For you as an individual. For your organization. Or for society as a whole. The solutions we propose can wreak serious havoc if questions and answers are left unchecked. For example, how will we ensure financial stability, healthcare, and security for those perpetually "otherwise" employed (ding ding . . . freelancers)? How can we ensure access and support for reskilling to everyone, not just the privileged few? How will we keep inherent bias out of the algorithms that increasingly control our lives?

The answer, is we must understand the principles in this book in their entirety—not just sound bites. As product leaders building this future, we lose sleep over the implications this technology can have. Our nightmare would be replacing a bad model with something even worse.

But before we get too worried about what could go wrong, let's take stock of where we stand today and recognize that there's a relative Pareto Principle for us changemakers in work—20 percent of companies and individuals are beautiful while 80 percent are crap. Let's work to make the beautiful 20 percent the norm, not the exception.

THE PROBLEMS WITH TODAY'S WORKPLACE— THE EMPLOYEE'S PERSPECTIVE

As changemakers, we spend a lot of time looking up. We take on too much responsibility. Take big risks. And we don't necessarily overpromise, but we're certainly not immune to biting off more than we can chew. Which leaves us vulnerable to toxic organizations or to individuals looking to climb their way to the top. Yet it's not just the ground floor that leaves us feeling trapped. The more power we get, the tighter the handcuffs (even though they're "golden"). We have resources. We have influence. Yet the resources can feel more like a burden. And the influence will never be free from "the boss" at the top. Thus, whether at the bottom, in the middle, or even at the top, the promise of a *Harvard Business Review* article can feel out of touch once the reality of an anxiety-inducing cesspool of poor behavior and incompetence becomes the reality of work.

Let's play a game of "never have I ever." Never have I ever . . . raise your hand if you've ever had any of these happen to you (it's okay, the people sitting next to you on the train won't think you're weird).

- *Showed up in a meeting to see your boss presenting your work as his own.* He gets the attaboy and promotion, and you fetch his coffee. In the meantime, he's using corporate assets and resources to start his side business.

- *Been berated by a screaming, cussing manager in front of your peers.* You still count yourself lucky because your colleague is getting an even bigger dose of verbal and emotional abuse.

- *Spent months perfecting an email and presentation to present an idea to the VP.* Then, after mind-numbing reviews and rewrites to nail the three minutes you have in front of her, she's mute and lifeless, probably fantasizing about driving her Porsche convertible down the coastal freeway. Then, months later, you're forwarded an email chain to answer a question, and when scrolling down the chain, you see that this same VP presented your slides and claimed them as hers. Did she like the idea? Loved it! So long as it was hers and not yours.

- *Been expected to be at your desk from eight to five every day, scheduled into meeting after meeting, and forced to respond to emails within minutes or fear the wrath of "I'll cc your boss and VP."* (As I write this during the evening, I was just pinged with one of these must-answer-now emails. Should I respond? I'll risk getting fired.) You don't have enough time during the day to focus, so you stay up late to get your real job done.

- *Worked your ass off "paying your dues" to demonstrate hard work, intelligence, empathy, and loyalty.* Then, in return, you are paid under market value. And instead of getting promoted, you watch a hotshot MBA grad or boomerang who left the company, founded a competitive startup, then was acquired back into the company making twice what you are.

- *Showed up for a company town hall to learn your boss and mentor is let go, you've been moved (yet again) to another manager, and your job will be changing.* You find this out along with everyone else, forced to grieve publicly, then sit through another hour-long presentation. You realize that this was actually in the works for the last year, yet you, your managers, and even your director were completely in the dark.

- *Received a text from an out-of-town partner asking if you're coming to dinner on Thursday.* When you ask them what's the occasion, you find out your leadership is having secret meetings . . . even though you've been running the relationship for the past year. It gets worse. The next month you find out this same leader told a partner every inquiry can only be run through them. Why? Who knows . . . all you know is you lost a friend. And whatever little trust you had in leadership.

- *Been told that you are not allowed to speak publicly or publish blogs, articles, books, and such, even if it's only tangential to your work.* You obediently follow, only to find out that your boss's boss did all those things.

- *Showed up in a client meeting full of white guys, many of whom are more junior than you, and the CEO instantly requests that you—the only woman in the room—take the notes.* Your boss calls you a "honey badger" (not a compliment) for being aggressive, while the male counterpart is called "assertive." You are patronized ("mansplaining"), harassed, passed over.

Is your hand still down? If you're one of the lucky few to have never experienced anything like these, congratulations! And please ask your company if they're hiring.

THE PROBLEMS WITH TODAY'S WORKPLACE— THE MANAGER'S PERSPECTIVE

It's comfy to think that we miserable individual contributors are bearing the brunt of the work while corporate fat cats sit back and rake in the bucks. As someone who now sits in the C-suite, I know that not to be true. The company and management are often just as miserable.

Toxic culture and people infect every part of the organization, sucking others into their orbit and making well-meaning people miserable—sometimes miserable enough to quit. You try to fix it with feedback, social events, quarantining toxic people, even firings, but it's like whack-a-mole—knock one down and three more pop up.

Entire divisions are inadvertently pitted against each other due to misaligned incentives, leading to resistance, finger-pointing, and even open hostility. You go through reorg after reorg (the yearly "November Classic"), but as you optimize for one issue, you sub-optimize others, and the problems persist. It's whack-a-mole again.

Outdated hierarchies and lack of transparency lead to grown adults treating other grown adults like children. Managers are privy to information that their "underlings" are not supposedly sophisticated or mature enough to handle. That goes up the stack too: senior executives don't share a lot of information with their managers. You try to go against the grain and empower your team with more information, but 90 percent of them are bored and uninterested, faces buried in their phones.

The majority of your job time is spent on unfulfilling busy work: HR self-assessments that have zilch to do with reviews, raises, bonuses, and career progression (management's already preordained all that). Reading that thirtieth email in a thread about something you're only tangentially involved in. (Hey, you wanted transparency!) Expense reports. PowerPoints. Team meetings. One-on-one meetings. Project status meetings.

But at least you've made it to the top. Things are awesome, right? Sure, you're making a sh**-ton of money. But when you hit the C-suite, you find yourself isolated from the social networks that used to make work tolerable.

By the time problems hit your level, all the easy and even medium ones are out of the way, leaving only the most complex, existential issues that inundate you day in and day out.

And if you think that other C-suites will treat you nicer and with some respect, you're wrong again. You will still be on the receiving end of cuss-laden yell-fests.

Mo' money, mo' problems.

When it comes to the problems that plague companies and employees, it's not entirely the managers' fault (although they can change and be changemakers in their own right). You can't entirely blame them for the culture and situation that breeds this bad behavior. Take, for instance, the now-famous Stanford prison experiment. Psychology professors organized a simulation that divided college students randomly into prison guards and prisoners to see how situations affect people's behavior (the old nature-versus-nurture argument).

Professor Philip G. Zimbardo says of the experiment: "Our planned two-week investigation into the psychology of prison life had to be ended after only six days because of what the situation was doing to the college students who participated. In only a few days, our guards became sadistic and our prisoners became depressed and showed signs of extreme stress."

Even well-intentioned people (and I do believe many moving into management are good people with good intentions) can be corrupted by power and a management structure that breeds bad behavior.

FROM BAD TO UNBEARABLE

Sure, work has been broken for a while. This isn't new information. Movies, spoofs, and memes have existed for decades now. But things are different today. Work is not only *not fun*, but it's coming apart at the seams. Pension plans collapse. Mass layoffs. College grads and middle-aged professionals find themselves strangely in the same boat—unemployed and seemingly unemployable. Even when times seem better and the economy is chugging, the aggregate numbers hide despair and disparity. And with each recession, jobs and lives are lost that will never recover.

What changed? Technology slashed the defining advantage of large companies: being large. It used to be that having a great idea wasn't enough. You needed access to resources that only large companies could afford—money and capital-intensive equipment. Yes, keeping large organizations running is tough. It comes with a lot of red tape, mediocrity, and inefficiencies. But because of the transactional costs of business, the sheer size of a large company was more effective than what small groups could do.

Then came the cloud. With the cloud, the world turned into one computer with billions of devices connected to it. By this time, I was a large company executive, jealous that startups no longer had the same barriers to entry. Startups could whip something up in weeks or months that would take us large companies years, whether it involved bringing products to market, updating existing products, or even emerging technologies (so-called greenfield, blue ocean, or horizon three innovations). Then when the startup gained traction, they could use cloud services like Amazon Web Services (AWS) to scale quickly in lockstep with customer demand.

This fundamental shift in technology from a scarcity-led to an abundance-based world is the reason for an outdated management model that's taken the office from bad to unbearable. And the results are dire for all of us. As early-career changemakers, we feel used and abused. As mid- to late-career changemakers, we feel trapped. Yet for all of us, it's no wonder there is a lack of loyalty and trust on both sides. We're talking a deep structural misalignment, an epidemic.

TIME FOR A SEA CHANGE

Every bully eventually meets their match. Goliath met David. Scut Farkus met Ralph in the movie *A Christmas Story*. Johnny had Daniel in *The Karate Kid*. And the office has the human and machine clouds.

Yesterday when the bully came knocking, we'd be stuck handing over lunch money and saying, "Thank you, sir, may I have another?" But we won't put up with it anymore because today we have another option.

Meet Sharon. When her brother died unexpectedly and she needed uninterrupted leave to be there for her family, her boss kept scheduling her for meetings. Instead of jumping into the repressed grief for prioritizing work over family, she jumped into the human cloud, and now handles bookkeeping for thirty-six companies, bringing in $26,000 a month, on her own time. As she said, "Not having an employer over my head is the most liberating feeling in the world."

Or Sam. After climbing the corporate ladder from software developer to VP of a $40 million business division, she left the workforce to raise her kids. When her kids went to college and she was ready to jump back in, a recruiter told her, "I'm going to be honest. You've been out of the workforce too long. No one is going to hire you." Like Sharon, Sam jumped into the human cloud, and instead of never being hired, she was earning six figures in just a few years. But deeper than the money, she's unlocked a way to work that's truly impactful. As she said of the human cloud compared to the office, "I wouldn't have been as involved in so many lives if I worked in a full-time role. I don't think I could ever work in an office again."

These are just two incredible individuals embracing the transformational change in front of us.

Now it's your time.

CHEAT SHEET

Lesson 1: The office wasn't built for us changemakers. We can all relate to stories of an anxiety-inducing cesspool of poor behavior and incompetence. It doesn't just feel broken when looking up; it feels broken whether you are an entry-level employee or sitting in the C-suite.

Lesson 2: The office has gone from bad to unbearable since today's disruption threatens to make the office obsolete.

Lesson 3: We no longer have to take it because the human and machine clouds are replacing the office (the sh** part at least).

WE DARE YOU

Activity 1: Make your own "never have I ever" with your work experiences. Do themes or recurring experiences pop up?

Activity 2: Ask yourself:

- Do I wake up every morning excited to go to work?
- Would I wake up early on a Saturday morning to work?
- If money didn't matter, would I be doing the same thing I do right now?

If your answer is *no* to any of the above, the rest of this book will give you the tools to turn these into a *yes*.

Activity 3: Read about the exponential change in technology over the past fifty years so that you can understand why the office has gone from bad to unbearable. Specifically, read about Moore's Law, Metcalfe's Law, and our brain's inability to decipher linear versus exponential change.

BOOKS WE RECOMMEND

The Industries of the Future by Alec Ross

The Inevitable: Understanding the 12 Technological Forces That Will Shape Our Future by Kevin Kelly

WTF? What's the Future and Why It's Up to Us by Tim O'Reilly

The Zero Marginal Cost Society: The Internet of Things, the Collaborative Commons, and the Eclipse of Capitalism by Jeremy Rifkin

2

RISE OF THE CHANGEMAKER

THE FUTURE BELONGS TO *YOU*
AND YOUR UNIQUE, EMPOWERED, DIGITAL SELF

Dear Future Employer,

Thanks for the "offer," but I'm going to have to pass. You see, I don't need you. Not anymore. I found a better way. I'm going to go out, make the world a better place, and work how, when, and with whom I want. Maybe I'll found a startup. Maybe I'll hop from project to project. Maybe I will join a company—just one that doesn't look anything like yours, one that actually functions and treats people like people. So, take your office, your salary, and your Kool-Aid, and go find someone else. Good luck with that.

Sincerely,

The Changemaker

In this new world we find ourselves in, we can finally reply to that social contract the way we've always wanted to. Your grandpappy wishes he could have done so. Now you can.

The power has shifted from the company to the individual. We can now access resources—people, tools, knowledge, and raw computing power—directly, without layers of middlemen taking their cut. What used to be managed by dozens of people is now handled by software. And what used to cost millions is nearly (and sometimes entirely) free.

Before, companies managed these factors of production, but today, individuals wield that power. Whether we're working in a company or on our own, we are the ones in the driver's seat. If companies are to survive, they will need to reorganize around you, the changemaker, instead of the other way around.

What does that look like in practice? Take my own experience. I'm a bit of a wannabe Renaissance person. I love to write. And play music. And create art. And program software. And . . . you get the point. But I had to specialize or risk being unemployed, so I went down the technology route and climbed the (mostly) traditional corporate ladder.

Today, though, I use human cloud platforms like Upwork to scratch my various creative itches. I ghostwrite, build analytics software, and do consulting engagements, all from the comfort of my home office before my regular workday begins. I communicate through G Suite and Trello, use open-source tools to build software, and get paid through the platform, without me needing to worry (too much) about bookkeeping and finance. The gigs are less about the money for me and more about how they create the opportunity to do exciting work I wouldn't otherwise be doing.

It's all possible because of two trends that are transforming the way we work: the human and machine clouds.

RISE OF THE CLOUDS

So, what exactly are the human and machine clouds?

The *human cloud* is the platform by which people and businesses can easily and quickly find and work with other people in a digital, remote, and outcome-based way. Consider it the "office in the cloud" since it translates everything that happens in a physical office through a digital equivalent.

Take building a mobile application. You need to hire the right people. Pay these people. Assign tasks. Share files. Answer questions. Provide feedback. Send dog memes. Everything that working in a physical office requires . . . just in a 100 percent digital and remote way.

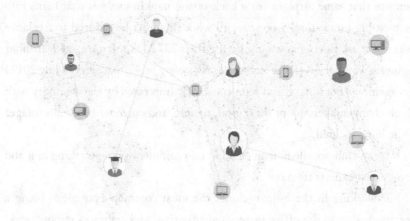

Physical Office versus Human Cloud

TASK	PHYSICAL OFFICE	HUMAN CLOUD
Hire	HR Department	Human Cloud Platform
Pay People	Finance Department	Human Cloud Platform
Assign Tasks	Office Drive-bys,* In-Person Stand-ups, Spreadsheets	Trello, JIRA, Asana
Share Files	Email, Looking at a Colleague's Computer	Google Drive, Microsoft Teams, Dropbox, Box
Answer Questions	Office Drive-bys, Meetings, Email	G Suite (in document), Trello, JIRA, Asana, Microsoft Teams, Slack
Provide Feedback	Office Drive-bys, Meetings, Email	G Suite (in document), Trello, JIRA, Asana, Microsoft Teams, Slack
Send Dog Memes	Office Drive-bys, Email	Slack

*This applies to every scenario where someone walks into your office. For me, I clocked an office drive-by every thirteen minutes, for everything from a joke, to a question, to just saying hi.

Let's be clear, offices won't fully go the way of the dinosaurs. Just like how not all organizations are bad eggs, there are some great things about the physical office. Where else can you throw a paper airplane at your coworker, then use that same airplane for a back-of-the-napkin analysis that turns into the next big innovation? Likewise, all work shouldn't be reduced to freelance tasks—just ask Boeing how outsourcing their 737 Max software to $9-an-hour engineers worked out. (Peter Robison at *Bloomberg* broke that story in July 2019.) But again, it's not binary, and I am constantly impressed by the creativity with which changemakers adopt the digital, remote, and outcome-based advantages of the human cloud.

We can embrace the human cloud in two common ways—working in it and hiring other experts from it.

For working in the human cloud, the most common example is being a freelancer. But, as the office increasingly digitizes and embraces remote work, we'll all work like freelancers. This means we'll all control where we work, when we work, and what we work on. For example, a month before this manuscript was due, I spent a week in China to focus. Is that a little over the top? Probably. But having a week where everything is blocked and the only thing I recognize is a Starbucks logo was definitely my best productivity hack yet (and the bao was great).

For hiring experts in the human cloud, what would you do if you had a world of experts in your pocket? Think five-star designers, developers, data scientists. Would you build that app you've been thinking about? Or write that article you've drafted? Or just design the leadership deck you're probably procrastinating on right now? You name it, and so long as it can be done as a project, an expert is waiting to help you. (Hint: *Everything* can be done as a project.)

As you'll soon see, the human cloud works whether you're an army of one, a small team or startup, or even a large corporation (when done correctly). I've embraced it as an individual to build a textbook. That was simple—one expert designer out of Nashville, Tennessee. I've embraced it in a large organization to build a product, bring it to market, then scale to the point of organization-wide investment. That was complex, with five to fifteen freelancers at one time integrated within teams of ten to fifty full-time employees, spanning sales, marketing, and product development (spread over five time zones). While these two experiences seem very different, they both are driven by seamless access to talent and work outcomes, no matter your station or situation in life.

The *machine cloud* is the yin to the human cloud's yang. Instead of accomplishing tasks with only humans, the machine cloud can perform or support many tasks through automation and artificial intelligence (AI). Straightforward tasks (and increasingly complex ones too) are handled by machines, freeing you up for the really meaty work. It's not just about saving the time of the task itself but also the mental switching cost of going from simple task to simple task.

Imagine having a virtual automated assistant that plans your calendar, helps draft your emails, conducts research for you, and even manages your social media accounts. What if I told you those tools exist today? (Because they do.)

Take Ajay Goel, for instance, an entrepreneur who built a marketing tool called GMass that helps send and manage emails for small and medium businesses. Or Andrew Arruda, CEO and founder of ROSS Intelligence, an AI-enabled legal research assistant powered in part by IBM Watson technology.

But it's not all about the tech. We also hear from people like Cat Casey and Gordon Shotwell, who both have liberal arts backgrounds but found their way to the machine cloud through a shared ability to fulfill the needs of humans with the capabilities of machines. They sit squarely at the intersection of these two clouds. Talk about changemakers.

DIGITAL YOU

In the office, we're just a number (quite literally). We have a seat, title, and short job description. We learn office "norms," play the politics, bounce from meeting to meeting, all while looking busy by pushing things around, often without actually creating anything.

But the human and machine clouds create a fundamentally different relationship between work and us. We're no longer just a box beholden to office politics. And we can no longer hide behind that job title and short list of responsibilities. Today we're naked, with our track record visible for the world to see.

In the Introduction we mentioned J Cheema, a designer based in Portland, Oregon, who left a lucrative role at Nike to work through the human cloud platform Upwork. Google his name, and you'll get back a list of impressive reviews:

- "J Cheema designed a VERY boring and complicated schematic in a clever and easy to understand way, in an animated PPT slide. Great strategic thinker!"—**High-End Executive PowerPoint presentation to be the keynote at conference, $350**
- "Excellent and professional work done with thoughtful input and an eye for detail."—**Expertise in Graphic Designing for an Investor Presentation, $500**
- "I have been working with J for over six months. He is the first person I go to when I have a presentation I want to make excellent. He has great vision, very strong design and graphic chops, and he's great to work with. A strong communicator and capable project manager."—**Startup Pitch PPT, $1,290**
- "J Cheema completed great work in a very tight deadline at a short notice. His communication skills were very good and he was quick to reply. His skills and expertise were strong and he followed the brief to the letter and on point."—**Fixing up design for PowerPoint, $250**

Click on one of these reviews, and you'll also find tangible artifacts of the relevant and past presentations.

Now, think about your own Google search. Since you're a changemaker, you probably have just as much praise, if not more, than J (sorry, J!). You've also built some really cool stuff that other potential employers or collaborators would love to see. But does your performance and hard work pop up on Google? Or is it hidden in a corporate feedback system?

The human cloud thinks playing hide-and-seek with your merit is unfair. Which is why it puts every single one of us on one network that's global, transparent, and quantified.

Imagine if every single one of us looked like a product on Amazon (but in the most humanistic and empowering way possible). Ratings. Reviews. Even real-life examples.

Ada Lovelace
iOS & Android App Development

98% job success

$ 130.00/hr Capital. CA

Ada had a very methodological approach that fit well with our team. She also went the extra mile with every milestone
- Jocelyn L

Ada was a self - starter that needed very little direction to deliver high quality work - Gary J

★★★★★
(73)

MORE REVIEWS

Well, we already are there. The reason is that software is shifting our relationship with work from being physically present in real-world local networks (think within an hour of your home and office) to being digitally present in a virtual, global, limitless network (the internet and relevant applications). We used to be connected to a handful of people close to us. Today, we can be connected with people across the globe with all sorts of experiences and expertise. We become much more powerful digitally present "nodes" in this network, augmented by the people and technology we connect with.

I know . . . that's pretty meta. So, what exactly is a node?

Node (noun): a point at which lines or pathways intersect or branch;
a central or connecting point.

We already experience this with social networks. We all have a page, a profile, a virtual avatar that mimics our physical self. This "digitization" is now happening in our professional lives, replacing what once lived on a paper resume with what now lives on our digital profile.

If your head is spinning, that's good. This transformation isn't incremental. And the implications are far more impactful than getting a "like" from your crush. But these implications aren't evenly distributed. They disproportionately benefit *you*, which is why the rise of the changemaker is replacing the traditional office.

RISE OF THE CHANGEMAKER

The shift from boxes on an org chart to digital nodes is driving the rise of the changemaker in four ways.

I. We Have the Power and Autonomy to Shape Our Careers

Think of work like buying a used car. Pre-internet, your local car dealership had the power. They controlled the price, terms, even the knowledge of whether the car was a dud. As Daniel Pink said in *To Sell Is Human: The Surprising Truth about Moving Others*, it was a *caveat emptor*, "buyer beware" world. Then came the internet, and all of a sudden, every car was put onto one platform, with crowdsourced ratings and reviews rather than the used car salesperson's word. It became a *caveat venditor* world, "seller beware."

The office is the car dealership in this analogy. It's losing its power. The world is no longer "employee beware." It's an "employer beware" and "manager beware" world. Treat us right or we'll leave. Obviously not everyone can quit their job today. Or even voice concern for fear of losing their paycheck. But as you'll learn, we can embrace the human cloud in unique ways suited for individual situations.

And it's not just treating us right while working together. We'll know if you're a piece of garbage before we even start. Consider Rate My Professors. I owe the shaping of my college experience to prior students' ratings and reviews of professors. Before deciding on a class, I knew if the professor cared about their students or if they were the type to make students buy their own textbook. It was so empowering. Now in the human cloud, managers are held accountable like those professors.

2. We Don't Need to Be Executives to Produce Outcomes at Scale

Unfortunately, we can't do it all. We can't know everything, and even if we did, we need sleep. In the office, the solution is having the biggest army, the most "head count."

But the human and machine clouds shatter this dynamic by slashing the friction of finding, hiring, paying, and working with talent. These activities used to require their own departments—HR, Finance, Procurement. Now, individuals can do all this through a simple checking account. This means we all have the power of an executive, without needing to have a large dedicated team. Laszlo Nadler used the human cloud to outsource his entire supply chain and create a one-person million-dollar planner business. Ajay Goel used the machine cloud to build a successful company and life around an email plug-in in Gmail.

Changemakers don't need to "earn our stripes" by kissing ass until we get the corner office or become master delegators. We can tap into the help of experts. We can create and collaborate instead of delegate and dictate.

3. We Don't Need the Macho Hierarchy Because We Can Work as Self-Organizing Peers and Collaborators

We love the concept of collaborating, but let's face it: outside of touting some new-aged management consulting articles, the office still runs by top-down command-and-control leadership.

But the clouds rip apart this relationship. It's no longer a top-down "do as I say" mentality, but rather a flattened collaboration of peers, all experts in their own right, working to accomplish a larger vision. It truly is gestalt—the whole is greater than the sum of its parts. Instead of spending time focusing on verbal communication, clarity is driven by tools. (Just wait until you learn how to build this later in the book.)

4. We Can Wear Sweatpants

Okay, it's more about being able to work anywhere, at any time, on our own schedule, but comfort never hurts.

Why does a San Francisco coffee shop, coworking space, and even an office look like a basement full of middle schoolers? Sweatpants. Graphic T-shirts. Maybe people are wearing shoes?

Because it can, since the human and machine clouds rip apart everything ancillary to the actual work. I love the saying "code is king" because code doesn't care how you get something done. It only cares if the input (what you actually did) results in the intended output.

The difference today is that digital tools enable value to be captured from the work itself versus the ancillary politics signaling good work. For example, we've all had that colleague who sends the "good news" email about the work they did, claiming it a huge success, thanking a bunch of people, then hoping no one actually looks at the work itself. In the human cloud, there's no reason for the email because everything, from the tasks to the documents themselves, is 100 percent open and transparent. So, instead of "thank you, Susie" in an email, everyone can see the exact task that Susie did, the exact file Susie worked on, and even the exact feedback Susie received from various colleagues.

This is why Susie can trade her IBM blue suit for sweatpants and Birkenstocks. We can be uniquely us, and let the work speak for itself.

A WORD OF CAUTION

It's not all good news, though. The human and machine clouds don't inherently fix problems. If a problem isn't fixed, it can end up being amplified by the human and machine clouds. The promise and perils of technology are obvious and increasingly challenging.

The human and machine clouds are far from immune to these perils. As Benek Lisefski, a freelancer based in Auckland, New Zealand, said about younger generations jumping into freelancing: "Generations of young minds, tired of employment norms that no longer served their needs, thought gig working was their ticket to career freedom and meaningful work. Now they're realizing they've traded one prison for another."

The reason is that the human cloud isn't a magic pill. It just accentuates what we already value in work. We call it the *amplification effect*. If you're valuable in full-time employment, you will probably be more valuable, make more money, and have more control in a human cloud environment. But if you're not adding value in full-time employment—if you don't have the right skills (whether technical or soft), relevant experience, and a strong network—the human cloud won't help you. It may even make your life worse.

The freelance and AI trends specifically, and technology advancements in general, tend to create greater disparity between the haves and have-nots. Those with fewer socioeconomic and educational opportunities, as well as those subjected to sexism and racism, often end up on the losing end of the equation.

Regardless of your political stance, we need societal constructs that support opportunity for everyone in this new world, regardless of where they start. Basics that many of us take for granted, such as healthcare, child and elder care, and financial knowledge, need to be more commonplace and readily accessible. Otherwise, the gap between winners and losers in this new economy gets ever wider.

OUR ASK

As a changemaker, you inherently are a leader and your work and leadership significantly influence large amounts of people. Thus, before you continue reading and accept the challenge of embracing the human and machine cloud, ask yourself:

Do I accept responsibility for the societal implications of gutting a system we've accepted as normal for the past 150 years?

We're not just playing with bits of code or convincing someone to go to Bali instead of Miami. We're fundamentally altering the livelihoods of those we influence. And just as this world amplifies our own unique value, it amplifies the problems we face as a society. And let's face it—we have some serious problems. When individuals work for themselves, they don't have the ability to negotiate healthcare coverage. Likewise, accountants with student debt, Uber drivers, and the majority of the workforce can't pay for another degree or afford six months with no pay to attend a coding camp. This is just the tip of the iceberg.

Which is why we have the following asks before you continue.

Get in the arena. As Brené Brown says in *Dare to Lead*, "If you are not in the arena getting your ass kicked on occasion, I'm not interested in or open to your feedback." Reading this book will be the easy part. Go get your ass kicked.

Understand the whole before you pick and choose which parts resonate with you. Unfortunately, this transformation isn't the dollar menu. Before you order the number three, you have to understand each side of who's participating and who's affected by this change.

Think beyond the work. Think how we can transform work in a way that uplifts and empowers opportunity for everyone. Here is a hint . . . we will need portable benefits. We will need safety nets. We will need regulation. One creative solution for the racial bias in human cloud matching algorithms is taking out the name and face of applicants. What more can we do to make sure this change lifts the ocean and not just a couple of boats?

RELEASE THE CHANGEMAKER

We live in a world that history's greatest emperors could only dream of. We can order a chariot on our phone while sitting on the couch. Take that, Caesar.

In this new world, we can go beyond our own human brain and the backs of subordinates and, instead, plug into the human and machine clouds to exponentially increase our impact. It took hundreds of thousands of people decades to build the high-value companies of our parents: GE, AT&T, Procter & Gamble. Yet it only took sixteen people and two years for Instagram to be acquired for a billion dollars. Or one person to build a million-dollar business. And this is just the beginning.

The human and machine clouds are a changemaker's dream. To use geeky software terms, it's scalable. It can go from one user to a hundred users to a million users seamlessly. It's also customizable. It can mold to whatever purpose you need it to, whether you're a freelancer, a full-time employee, an entrepreneur, or a leader driving the human cloud within a company. And it's up for the taking.

Throughout this book, we seize this opportunity.

In the next section, we'll embrace the human cloud. We'll learn how to work in the human cloud so that we can control where we work, when we work, and what we work on, along with unlocking an accelerated opportunity feedback loop. We'll then learn how to tap into the human cloud so that we can unlock outcomes at scale by hiring freelancers and teams of freelancers. Then, we'll build organizations around the human cloud, unlocking external talent and increasing our own employee engagement.

In the machine cloud section, we'll embrace advanced technology to accomplish tasks through automation and artificial intelligence.

Finally, we'll release our changemaker by building the mindset that unlocks the consistent and long-term execution of applying these clouds.

We can't promise you the world, but we can promise you a means to make your dent in it.

CHEAT SHEET

Lesson 1: We as individuals don't need the company anymore because we now own the factors of production. Rather than needing to work in an office, we can now tap into the human and machine clouds.

- **Human Cloud:** The "office in the cloud," a platform by which people and businesses can easily and quickly find and work with other people in a digital, remote, and project-based way.

- **Machine Cloud:** Accomplishing or supporting tasks through automation and artificial intelligence.

Lesson 2: We're no longer hidden behind the corporate firewall. We're naked in a global network, and our value has shifted from being a number incentivized for conformity to creating our unique digital profile.

Lesson 3: Four forces are driving the rise of the changemaker.

1. We now have the power and autonomy to shape our careers.

2. We don't need to be executives. We can remain the creator and create outcomes at scale.

3. We don't need the macho hierarchy because we can work as self-organizing peers and collaborators.

4. We can trade the blue suits for sweatpants because it's about the work, not the ancillary things like dress and office politics.

Lesson 4: The human and machine clouds amplify what we already value. If you're doing poorly in full-time employment, you're probably doing even worse in the human and machine clouds.

WE DARE YOU

Activity 1: Buy something on Amazon, then ask yourself, "Why did I purchase this?" Then imagine you were the product on Amazon. What would your product be? Who would hire you?

Activity 2: Search yourself on Google. What pops up? Pictures from a college party or your unique human product on Amazon?

Activity 3: Conduct a virtual work audit to understand if the work you do could and should be done in a remote environment. How? Go to the coffee shop, go to a coworking space, or stay at home instead of going into the office for a week. What do you find yourself doing? Are you more productive? Are you adding more value (producing more or having higher-quality work)? If yes, good! If no, why not? Is the actual work not conducive to being done virtually? If the work is conducive, then what factors does an office provide for you that virtual does not (*hint* . . . most likely a coworking space can provide this)?

Activity 4: Read about the implications of today's technology trends to understand the paradigm shifts in work.

BOOKS WE RECOMMEND

New Power: How Power Works in Our Hyperconnected World—and How to Make It Work for You by Jeremy Heimans and Henry Timms
The Future of the Professions: How Technology Will Transform the Work of Human Experts by Richard Susskind and Daniel Susskind
Humans Are Underrated: What High Achievers Know That Brilliant Machines Never Will by Geoff Colvin
The Second Machine Age: Work, Progress, and Prosperity in a Time of Brilliant Technologies by Erik Brynjolfsson and Andrew McAfee

THE
HUMAN
CLOUD

3

RISE OF THE HUMAN CLOUD

THE ENGINE MAKING WORK BETTER

Let me tell you about my dystopia.

For five days a week, around fifty weeks out of the year, I go to the same spot, for the same amount of time, and do the same thing day in and day out, with little to no control.

Wait, that's not a dystopia—that's just work.

I'll never forget the day I learned this sad reality. I was on the thirty-second floor of a high-rise in Boston, excited beyond excited since many sleepless nights went into getting this opportunity.

Prior to this, I had worked on a project-to-project basis out of coffee shops, helping small businesses and startups with anything business-related—market research, accounting, business planning, literally anything I could teach myself through YouTube. While I absolutely loved it, I didn't think it was work. Geeky I know, but I considered it fun. But everyone around me told me to get a "real" job with salary and benefits. So, I couldn't wait to start what everyone told me was the dream job, being a partner-track analyst at a Big Four accounting firm.

But a couple weeks in, I had a near panic attack. After experiencing both ways of life, the *real* world totally sucked. People walked around like zombies, pointing to everything besides actual work to justify their existence. The perks. The logo. The upcoming happy hour. I felt like I was learning the truth about Santa Claus all over again—except this lie would affect the rest of my life.

WHY THE HUMAN CLOUD

While for me this "reality" totally sucked (#firstworldproblems), it was a privilege that it was even possible. Sharon Heath, a bookkeeper living in Virginia Beach, had to choose between work or family when Sharon's brother died unexpectedly at age thirty-five.

Sharon's family was thrown into a state of grief and turmoil unlike anything they had ever experienced. Sharon needed to coordinate the funeral logistics and be there for her family in Massachusetts. So, she dropped everything and returned to her family home.

Meanwhile, her company kept scheduling and expecting her to show up for meetings, without any regard for her terrible situation.

I'm sure it's a feeling most of us can relate to, though perhaps not on such a drastic level as Sharon's. Whether trying to take a vacation, catch your kid's soccer game, or care for an ailing family member, companies often pressure us to put them first. For me, I just wanted to take my first-ever vacation after a year and a half with the company. I told leadership I'd be off the grid for two weeks and needed that time to clear my head. I hopped on a plane to Asia, and the second I landed, I had an email from leadership. It was a question they could've simply found on the spreadsheet I built for them, but it was easier to bug me. Respect . . . shattered.

But Sharon worked up the courage to voice her need for space and time. Since she had recently received a stellar performance review and a raise, it seemed like a simple ask. Her employer reacted positively at first, then quickly went back to expecting her to put the company over her family.

For Sharon, something inside her finally snapped. This crossed the line. So, with grief hanging over her and her employer's demands in mind, she quit her job and jumped straight into the human cloud.

WHAT IS THE HUMAN CLOUD

The human cloud is a term that's sexy and makes headlines. We, as an industry, like to throw buzzwords out there to make it even more confusing. Gig economy. Freelance economy. Liquid workforce. Elastic networks. Open innovation. I feel like a curmudgeon wanting to scream from my front porch, "Everyone just shut the fu** up!"

The reason is that, beyond buzzwords, the human cloud is just *how* we work in the cloud. It's not a single tool or product. Rather, it's a collection of tools and applications transforming how we work, from one job with one physical office to a digital, remote, and outcome-based world.

For example, think about the two most common activities we consider work—communicating and collaborating. Do we still need one physical place to talk to each other, ask questions, share files, and ask for feedback? Or can we do this at a coworking space, your favorite coffee shop, your living room—or, in my case, literally a cloud (since I wrote this on a plane)?

Of course, we don't need one physical office, since not only does each activity have a digital equivalent, but the digital equivalent is proving better for productivity and creativity. If I were in an office right now, about thirteen minutes into working, a colleague would come into my office to tell me a joke or ask a question. We'd talk for thirty minutes, and by the time I looked back down at my computer, I'd be running late for my next meeting. I'd half pay attention in that meeting, trying to finish what I started before being interrupted. Then both the meeting and what I was working on would be semi-productive.

When packing up to go home, I'd stress about how nothing got done and how my night would turn into catch-up. And the cherry on top . . . I'd sleep for about four hours or be up all night thinking about the work I didn't finish. Now, extrapolate this to life in an open office . . . yikes! Meanwhile, in the human cloud, communication is on our terms. Need three hours with no distraction? Don't answer the Slack message. Or, leverage tools to optimize for your own workflow.

Unfortunately for Sharon, the ability to control her time wasn't an option. Let's face it, accounting jobs, like many others, aren't known for flexibility. Thus, she has a pretty tough predicament on her hands. How could she get safety and stability while achieving flexibility in a career not known for it? She wanted to have her cake and eat it too. So, how did the human cloud help?

OUR NEW OPPORTUNITY

Fortunately, Sharon knew about Paro, a human cloud platform for analysts, bookkeepers, CPAs, and CFOs.

Human cloud platforms are the digital matchmakers of the human cloud. They connect freelancers, also called independent talent, with those who need the talent, along with providing common support functions like contracting and payment processing.

You may think of a platform like Upwork (a merger of oDesk and Elance) or Freelancer.com. These were trailblazers, but they didn't invent freelancers. Technically, the term *free lances* goes back to medieval mercenaries who fought for whichever country paid them the most (yikes). And, there have been many models since the 1950s connecting freelancers with businesses—temp agencies, consulting agencies, and staffing firms. But early internet pioneers were the first to directly connect those doing the work with those needing the work, a model called direct-to-talent, effectively using software to cut out the middleman.

Traditionally if you were a freelancer, you would work for an agency, and the customer would contract with the agency, not you. This meant all the margins and control belonged to the agency. If you did well, the agency benefited. If you did poorly, the agency put someone else in. And if you did so well the customer wanted to hire you, the agency would block it unless the customer paid a big fee. Thus, this first leap—removing the middle layer between talent and those needing talent—really was monumental, and the next step was the human cloud.

For Sharon, joining Paro meant she had direct access to clients. She didn't have to handle finding clients or contracting. She could focus on being the best bookkeeper, which in return resulted in quickly earning $4,000 a month.

Connecting to clients around the globe is just one advantage of a human cloud platform. Software also enables communication and collaboration tools like G Suite, Trello, Slack, and JIRA, facilitating rapid, more efficient working relationships. These tools reduced the friction of all the ancillary tasks that go into work, enabling Sharon to focus on her actual work while making her working relationships feel more effective as a freelancer than when she was a full-time employee. She not only unlocked doors to new clients but was able to more meaningfully and efficiently manage a larger number of clients and projects.

With this combination in hand—easy to connect with clients, easier to work with clients—her demand skyrocketed tenfold within six months. The demand was so great that she turned her sole proprietorship into a family-operated S corporation, Gold Star Bookkeeping, and employed three people, including her husband and daughter.

She now handles bookkeeping for thirty-six companies, bringing in $26,000 a month. But it's not just about the money. She unlocked opportunity well beyond landing a better full-time job. She unlocked a mindset, or as she said, "If one decent thing came out of what happened with my brother, it's that it was a turning point for me. After he passed away, my thought process changed." And this mindset unlocked an opportunity beyond what one company could provide. "I would never go back to working for somebody. Not having an employer over my head is the most liberating feeling in the world. I make my own schedule. I choose the hours I work every day and what I work on. I choose the clients I want to work with, and the ones I don't."

HOW WE WILL EMBRACE THE HUMAN CLOUD

The story of Sharon is incredible. But it's not unique. It's the result of a paradigm shift in how we work from one job in one physical office to a digital, remote, and project-based world.

But. The human cloud is just a tool. *Not* a magic trick. Nor an "end." It is just a means, a medium for us changemakers to make a bigger dent in the world.

Sharon used the human cloud to help her family *and* have multiple streams of income that weren't location- or communication-dependent.

For me, the human cloud is a tool to accelerate my opportunity feedback loop and control where I work, when I work, and what I work on. I write this from a coffee shop in Singapore where the Wi-Fi is great and the food is even better. And, my best friend and I have a dumb tradition of running a half marathon here every December. So, why can't I visit him *and* work? Likewise, I tap into the human cloud to work with experts like Sharon on a project basis to help me accomplish more.

For you, the potential is limitless. There's no one right way to use it or one type of person who can use it. You can be a freelancer . . . entrepreneur . . . corporate manager and still embrace the human cloud.

We'll embrace this tool in three ways—working in the human cloud, tapping into the human cloud, and building organizations around the human cloud.

WORKING IN THE HUMAN CLOUD

Sharon taught us one way to use the human cloud as a tool—working in a fully digital, remote, project-based way. But working in the human cloud can take various forms. It's not *just* full-time freelancers. You'll soon read about Liane, who hops between freelance and full-time employment. Others freelance on the side, moonlighting to supplement full-time income or scratch an itch not being fulfilled in their day job. There will still be W-2 employees. But as the office increasingly transforms to digital, remote, and project-based, we will all start to work more like freelancers. The world is increasingly shifting into a human cloud work paradigm.

TAPPING INTO THE HUMAN CLOUD

Another way to embrace the human cloud is to hire experts from it to augment ourselves. We all have biological constraints. We can't know everything. And even if we do, we need sleep. The human cloud augments these biological constraints, enabling us to have experts and teams of experts at our fingertips.

Take the luckiest thing that ever happened to me—meeting Matt C. I was looking for someone to technically vet a report on artificial intelligence. I posted the project on Upwork for $150 and almost fell out of my chair upon seeing his profile. A CTO who built deep learning courses and who had a TED talk titled "AI as a Force for Good." Are you kidding me!? Within forty-eight hours of my posting the job, we started working together. And instead of the typical do-what-I-say assignment, we collaborated as equals, delivered a kick-ass report, and then built an ongoing relationship that led to the book you're reading today (and the hilarious picture below that his wife will forever be jealous of).

From left: Matthew Mottola, Matthew Coatney

I honestly still can't get over the potential of hiring experts from the human cloud. The fact that a twenty-five-year-old can hire a CTO by merely searching on Google is beyond comprehension. And it's not just him. (Sorry, Matt, you're still special to me.) I've hired designers, developers, management consultants, writers, editors, and project managers. You name the position, and I've likely hired for it. All without having a C in my title. And for most of it, while living in a living room in San Francisco.

BUILDING ORGANIZATIONS AROUND THE HUMAN CLOUD

But wait, there's more! Working and tapping into the human cloud are just a few of its superpowers. The human cloud isn't only for individuals. It's also for organizations—and organizations aren't going away any time soon. They'll trim, kind of like when April hits and you realize that winter weight won't work for beach season. But instead of disappearing, they'll focus on overcoming two monumental challenges—empowering changemakers like you not to leave every six months and keeping up with startups.

Let's be honest. We smart, hungry, disruptive change agents don't stay still for long. We need to be challenged, empowered, and given the resources to make sh** happen. Companies will need to find ways to provide you with the tools to make hay, or you'll go somewhere else that does. Enter the human cloud. In progressive companies, you'll be able to hire through the human cloud just like I was able to hire Matt C. Except instead of my personal checking account, you'll have the corporate account. And instead of a static title and job description, you'll be accountable to outcomes far beyond those three to five bullets in your job responsibilities. Take my hidden role of PM. Does it mean project manager or product manager? Hell if I know. But rather than handed-down job responsibilities, I was held to clear outcomes requiring skills far beyond my biological reach.

I talked before about how startups are eating large corporations' lunches. The human cloud can help them fight back. Call it fighting fire with fire. Whether building products, bringing products to market, or product updates, startups can do in months what takes organizations years. And the reason is that talent is both hard to find and hard to bring in. It's no secret there's a developer and data science shortage. And of the talent there is, if they are not scooped up by Google or Facebook, they're not hanging out where $15 organic avocado toast isn't a block away (sorry, Midwest).

For a beloved North American motorcycle manufacturer, this didn't mean they could ignore a digital experience for their riders. They needed a next-generation mobile application, but they didn't have the budget, gravitas, or time to recruit a top-notch, full-time development team. Instead, thanks to changemaker Brandon Bright, they embraced accessing experts in the human cloud, taking the traditional staff acquisition cycle from months down to days while getting the best engineers and product experts they could find anywhere in the world.

Given all these options, I can safely say that the human cloud can work for just about anyone in a professional role. Let's now jump in and see how it works in practice.

CHEAT SHEET

Lesson 1: The office doesn't work for everyone, which has set the stage for a different way to work. This chapter highlights the problems of the traditional office through Sharon Heath, a bookkeeper who couldn't both take care of her family and work a traditional job when her brother died suddenly.

Lesson 2: The solution to "work not working for everyone" is the human cloud. The human cloud is just *how* we work in the cloud. It's not one tool or one product. Rather, it's a collection of tools and applications transforming how we work from one job with one physical office to a digital, remote, and project-based world. For Sharon, by joining the human cloud platform Paro, she had access to remote, project-based clients, enabling her more flexibility (and more income) than she had in a traditional office.

Lesson 3: We will embrace the human cloud in three ways.

1. Working in the human cloud
2. Tapping into the human cloud
3. Building organizations around the human cloud

WE DARE YOU

Activity 1: Read about the rise of platform business models and part-time, temporary, and independent work to understand the context behind today's digital-first human cloud.

BOOKS WE RECOMMEND

Modern Monopolies: What It Takes to Dominate the 21st Century Economy by Alex Moazed and Nicholas L. Johnson

Platform Revolution: How Networked Markets Are Transforming the Economy—and How to Make Them Work for You by Geoffrey G. Parker, Marshall W. Van Alstyne, and Sangeet Paul Choudary

Temp: How American Work, American Business, and the American Dream Became Temporary by Louis Hyman

4

WHY CHANGEMAKERS ARE MOVING TO THE HUMAN CLOUD

OUR NEW PATH TO OPPORTUNITY

Whose idea was it to lock humans up in a cage for eight hours at a time? Maybe you think the free coffee is worth it? Or donut Fridays? For me, I just don't get it. I love coffee shops. Specifically, this one coffee shop on the water in my small hometown called Plum Island Coffee Roasters. I can bike there. I can go for a walk or grab a smoothie down the street when the two o'clock drag hits. And if it gets too noisy, well, my Air Pods are noise-canceling.

But while my reasoning is cute, the reality is that the ability to even work in an office is a privilege because, for some, the prospect of an office is not feasible. Whether it be 99 percent of the talent who don't live in a major city. Or talent who can't be in one place for eight hours a day, like working parents, those taking care of aging or sick parents, or humans not content being owned by the boss. The fact is that while we hear about accessibility and inclusivity in corporate slogans and PR headlines, the office isn't accessible or inclusive. If PR wants to speak the truth, the office is just intrusive and exclusive.

Fortunately, the human cloud disrupts this by enabling access to work wherever you have an internet connection. As a writer in Asia put it: "With the internet and vast source of collaborative tools, working on our virtual team was no more different than working with people in the same room. And, it's pretty amazing to be able to communicate, collaborate, and connect with people all over the world."

But this is just a minor piece of the opportunity it presents. My favorite laptop sticker says, "I'm twenty in dog, I mean gig years." The reason is that the human cloud shortens the time it takes to prove value, meaning what takes years in the traditional office may only take months in the human cloud.

Take one of my favorite projects—building out virtual communication and collaboration standard operating procedures (SOPs). This was several years ago when such technologies were much less ubiquitous than today. The client was 100 percent remote, with members on three different continents. Yet for four months, I worked with leadership and working teams to plan, test, and implement an infrastructure using G Suite, Trello, and Slack that worked for the organization. It also provided a tangible work artifact for me to point subsequent clients to (and use myself!). Best of all, I had a review from the CEO that said, "Matt is very easy to communicate with, adds valuable insights during meetings, and is process driven. We brought Matt on board to help us create SOPs for our primary service and internal communication. Matt was able to create and implement both in under six months. I would highly recommend Matt to any team that is looking for organized, scalable growth." This led directly to my next couple of opportunities!

This was my typical experience working in the human cloud. From helping clients with budgeting to operations and strategy consulting, each project had a bunch of responsibility, a ton of challenging problems, and a working relationship much different than my peers—cross-continent, cross-functional, and being accountable to executive-level decisionmakers. I'd be lying if I said working with executives was simple. But once I understood the pulse of an executive—busy, numbers-driven, and human just like you and me—working in the human cloud taught me interpersonal skills you simply can't learn in a classroom or textbook. And this was just one of the many skills fueling the greater reward of working in the human cloud—an accelerated engine of opportunity. That is why when I entered the corporate world at the age of twenty-six, I entered with what felt like more than ten years of management experience.

But don't take it only from me. Let me share the experiences of Noel, Sam, J, and Liane—experts who make me look like a slacker taking a nap in the back of the classroom.

THE NEW AMERICAN DREAM

Noel Arellano looks like a beacon of opportunity—a Dell Scholar at Texas A&M and first-generation four-year college student.

Yet Noel felt trapped. He was raised to work in a factory. Everything from his schooling to his peers, family, and community-support system was built around preparing him to work at Anheuser-Busch in Baytown, Texas. Thus, when Noel stepped on campus, instead of keg stands and frat parties, he was playing catch-up on foundational skills. For example, when most college students walk into Calculus, we take it for granted that they had Algebra 1 and other math classes that built a math foundation. Apply this to writing, science, and the various elective courses that assume some level of foundational understanding, and we can start to perceive why someone groomed to work in a factory wouldn't be on an equal footing. That is why Noel had to skip the keg stands just to get on equal ground.

As if catching up on his course load weren't enough, then came the reality of why students go to school in the first place—to get a job. Do you remember your first career fair? Sweaty palms. Awkward small talk. If only you could take a lap, drop your resume off at each booth, then rip your tie off as you exit. But you can't. Instead, you have to smile, have a good handshake, and position your past work in a way that excites the rep enough to put you in the special pile. But what if you don't have the right type of past work? Whether because you were playing catchup with school or you weren't exposed to relevant experiences. Well then, you're pretty screwed. Or in the words of Noel, "While others were talking to recruiters for over twenty minutes, I seemed to not even have twenty seconds."

Fortunately for Noel, shortly afterward, he saw a webinar for a human cloud platform focused on students—Parker Dewey. Noel signed up, sifted through opportunities, and, within a week, started his first micro-internship—a sales outreach project.

Micro-internships aren't exactly like normal internships. While typical summer interns, who receive a full-time offer, are rewarded with a trip to Disney or a Pitbull concert, Noel's internship led him to a second micro-internship. Then a third and a fourth, until before he knew it, he was embarrassed when people at career services knew him by his first name since he was invited to so many interviews.

But deeper than the work itself, each project provided an accelerated feedback loop for Noel to grow as a professional. As he said, "Each project has given me indispensable knowledge about myself and the real world that I otherwise would have never attained. It has been a lot of hard work where I have put in countless hours, but it has given me a new level of confidence in my abilities as a professional." He learned the tangible skill set required for the job and the interpersonal skills needed for any client-facing relationship. Things like how to deliver information to an extremely busy executive. Or how to efficiently ask questions and absorb constructive feedback. Best of all, he gained exposure to different roles, industries, and companies he might want to work for. He worked for startups. He worked for large companies. And instead of corporate Kool-Aid, he was shown the ropes realistically with each project—actual work outcomes that were quantified and powering the engine of his opportunity feedback loop.

THE TRADITIONAL PATH IS DEAD (BUT THERE IS HOPE)

Noel, and every one of us, is caught in a contradiction. Companies need good talent. Good talent needs good jobs. Yet the bridge is broken.

What gives? The American Dream is at a crossroads. The *old* American Dream—glad-handing and a paper resume—is dead. The *new* American Dream is working in the human cloud.

What's the difference? The human cloud doesn't play by the old world's rules. It doesn't have time for politics—kiss someone's ass, smile, then backstab. Nor the game—blast dozens of resumes with a generic cover letter, wait on pins and needles for months, and then either receive the generic mail, "We found a better fit," or the even more generic "Congrats" (only to quit six months later when the actual job is nothing like the job post). Unless you grew up in the right country club or went to one of the chosen schools, this game is increasingly out of reach.

Instead, the human cloud runs on outcomes. And it quantifies these outcomes through ratings, reviews, and tangible artifacts.

WE HAVE A NEW RESUME

Noel knew he wouldn't win the traditional resume game. Instead, he dove head-first into building a new kind of resume: think of it as a product listing on Amazon, albeit a much more creative and human-centered one.

A good product comes down to two things—being unique and actually working. Outside of the staples everyone needs, products on Amazon must be hyper-unique to stand out, draw attention, and fit a niche need for a specific purchaser. The beauty of the marketplace is even a niche product can find lots of people because of the scale of the platform. For example, I needed an ugly holiday sweater for work, something that was humorous, kitschy, and could double as a vehicle for embarrassing the kids on a ski weekend. Within five minutes, I found a nice red-and-white sweater with a white llama donning a poofy cap. Sold. Where else could such a match happen so quickly?

It's the same for us and employment. Outside of the few jobs that everyone needs, e.g., doctors, it's no longer enough just to have a fancy piece of paper from a university. Like on Amazon, we need to hyper-specialize. Take Erica Ciko Campbell, a writer we met on the Upwork platform who specializes in writing on Leonardo da Vinci. She's a kick-ass writer. And, she was hyper-unique to what we needed—a paragraph on da Vinci and his famous painting *The Vitruvian Man*. Think about how that could have played out in the old world of lifelong employment and companies. Finding her would have been damn near impossible.

To become unique, we need to understand ourselves and build around our unique selves. I always ask students, "What do you do or look at when you're bored? Does this gravitate around an industry? A skill? A type of company? Or a company itself?" This stuff is hard to learn in a classroom, but we'll give you the tools to uncover it in the next chapter.

Like on Amazon, it's also not just enough to say, "Hey, hire me! I know what I'm doing!" It's not enough to say you worked at Microsoft for two years. You need to produce outcomes that we can point to and say, "Hey, I did that. Want me to do that for you too?" It's more about street cred than a logo on your resume.

To prove products work, companies use case studies or demos. The human cloud captures ratings, reviews, and tangible assets. Instead of simply listing two years at ABC Consulting Company, it automatically prioritizes who and how you tangibly helped (ratings and reviews) and what you actually built (portfolio). In a corporate environment, when you leave, your merit stays with the company. But in the human cloud, what you build is forever yours.

The beauty of this new resume is that it benefits from the accelerated opportunity feedback loop. Just like a product can become viral, the human cloud turns your flywheel of opportunity. Or as Noel told us:

> I went from not being able to attain a single opportunity, let alone an interview, to having more than ten interviews and a handful of full-time job offers. I used this newly acquired confidence to land a full-time position when I graduated from Texas A&M University with my bachelor's of science in chemical engineering. This was all in one year. One year! It is insane for me to think how much my life changed with the right opportunity. I never would have imagined all this being possible. For me, the college-to-career transition had been one of the most difficult challenges in my life, but each project gave me indispensable knowledge about myself and the real world that I otherwise would have never attained.

Beautiful.

THIS NEW DREAM IS FOR EVERYONE

The human cloud helps more than those entering the workforce.

Take Samantha Mason, a kick-ass PM and editor. Life was great in the traditional path. She climbed the corporate ladder from software developer to VP of a $40 million business division at a publicly traded company.

Then her two sons were born, and Sam wanted to apply that same tenacity she brought to delivering products to raising her kids. So, she quit the corporate life. She dove headfirst into organizing $100,000 fundraisers, overseeing the chess club for k–12 students, and running a cooking school for high school and college students.

When her kids left for college, she was ready to jump back in, but she found the corporate world was not so welcoming. Even though she had recertified in the necessary areas, doors remained closed to her.

Undeterred (if you know Sam, you know she doesn't do well with hearing *no*), she turned to the human cloud through a somewhat unconventional, yet surprisingly effective, path. She reached out to the author of a book she used for her Professional Scrum Master certification. After many years, she knew good content when she read it. But a nonnative English speaker had written the book, so it wasn't as clear as it could be. To get her foot in the door, she reached out to the author, offering to edit the book for free if he listed her as editor. He reluctantly agreed. Fast-forward . . . a German publishing house picked up the book, and Boston University uses it as the recommended book in one of its Questrom School of Business classes. Street cred through tangible artifact and client review . . . check.

Later, she joined Upwork and landed a job editing home-improvement posts for a company. Sam didn't start out knowing exactly how to succeed in the online world or what her unique niche was, so she started modestly, earning $8 to $35 for jobs lasting an hour or two. That turned into helping people launch their own blogs and creating personal branding for clients to land their dream jobs, school admissions, and fellowships. With each project, Sam honed her skills and became stronger and more focused. She didn't have a specific niche but started developing an ideal client—technical and professional clients because of a shared language and work drive. As she told us, "It all happened so quickly. What was fascinating and exciting was meeting people who needed short-term help with a specific project. The funny thing is that, three years later, I'm still working with that home improvement company. What started as an $0 contract turned into a long-term job for over $10,000. And even visiting them in Spain! They welcomed me with open arms by the CEO taking my family, me, and their entire team to lunch."

She cautions, "I have to admit, however, that it wasn't always easy, especially in the beginning. Self-doubt is real throughout the entire process because freelancing has ebbs and flows. I went nearly a month without a new client and little repeat business. But finally, I learned to take advantage of that opportunity to improve my website, write posts, reach out to previous clients, and take time for myself. I've learned that it's better to be patient than to rush into a potentially toxic job."

After three years of embracing the human cloud, Sam knows that she found a world better than the one she originally wanted to reenter. Does she work more? Yep. Does she still work weekends? Absolutely, but she does it because she wants to. Recently, a client needed her to finish a rush resume, which is often the case when someone is looking for a job. She said, "'The only time I have is 8:00 to 10:00 a.m. on Sunday. Take it or leave it.' The client took it at an increased rate." She went from being told no one would hire her to building a sustainable, lucrative freelance career. And, deeper than the income, she's made so many contacts around the world who will be lifelong friends. "I've worked with moms and their sons, dads and their daughters, and been privy to a wedding engagement. I've helped entrepreneurs start their businesses, connected them with attorneys to file patents, had an off-site at my house, and was in attendance when a startup presented to a VC I connected them with. Yes, I've seen the ups and downs, but I've witnessed people going after their dreams. I wouldn't have been as involved in so many lives if I worked in a full-time role. I don't think I could ever work in an office again."

For both Noel and Sam, the traditional nine-to-five path didn't work, but the human cloud did.

EVEN THOSE WHO CAN'T AFFORD TO DREAM

What if Sam never wanted to leave the workforce? If instead of being a kick-ass mom *or* working a full-time job, she wanted to be a kick-ass mom *and* work a full-time job? That's the case with presentation designer J Cheema.

J was beyond qualified for the corporate ladder at Nike. He had a BS from Johns Hopkins and an MBA from UNC-Chapel Hill (way smarter than us). He was chief of staff to a leadership team of twenty-six vice presidents in nine countries at Nike. He also served as Staff & Strategic Planning Director of Emerging Markets. Yet the higher he climbed, the more he lost control over what really mattered—his family.

So, instead of trading memories for corporate miles, J asked himself, "What if I could become my own boss and spend more time with my family?"

Just like Sam, J didn't wake up with a six-figure income thanks to this epiphany. Nor did he push a button and magically earn six figures with no corporate overlord. Even though he was a highly touted director, he still had to identify what was unique about him and build his street cred. In thinking about his unique differentiation, he reflected on his quirky skill at Nike—making PowerPoints—and he wondered if this could be his niche. He had a solid foundation with his MBA and his chief of staff and strategic planning director pedigree, and he clearly had management/strategy consulting skills. But what really differentiated him was his ability to take that strategy pedigree, along with a keen eye for design when it came to executive-level large organization requirements, and turn that into kick-ass decks.

He set his rate at $100 an hour and waited. He jokes, "That lasted about three days. I realized I had no experience on the platform even though I had more experience than most people. It was humbling not to receive any offers. So, I dropped my rate." J learned the hard way about street cred. He needed those quantified work artifacts with reviews to be taken seriously. So, while it wasn't easy and in a uniquely J manner, he lowered his fee to $30 since, "We had a nanny at the time for our son, and we paid her $20 an hour" (lolz).

Like Sam and Noel, it paid off. Today, J charges $250 an hour and has made over $350,000 as a freelance presentation designer. He is one of Upwork's top freelancers, working with brands like ExxonMobil, Microsoft, YouTube, GE, Nasdaq, Blue Nile, LinkedIn, Adidas, Revolution Growth, and Siemens. But deeper than any impact on his pocketbook, according to J, "I decide on my clients and projects and choose when and where to work. I'm in complete control of my day."

So, whether entering the workforce, reentering the workforce, or making work work for you, the New American Dream can work for everyone.

FROM THE HUMAN CLOUD TO CORPORATE

From the outside, Liane Scult looks like every other seasoned corporate veteran. A white Audi. An eco-friendly home in the burbs. But under the surface, Liane has a secret. While she looks like a typical corporate manager, at heart she works like she's in the human cloud.

The reason is that, before working in the human cloud was cool, Liane was an independent contractor. She didn't have a global network of potential projects since the human cloud wasn't built yet. But she worked project by project, with no steady salary or benefits package.

Similar to Sam, when Liane's kids were born, she knew working under the watch of a corporate overlord wasn't the environment she wanted to raise her kids in. She wanted to be at the bus stop for them. She wanted to attend every one of their soccer games (without missing her daughter's winning goal because she was multitasking with a meeting). But she also needed to work, so she connected with a temp agency that facilitated a six-month project management role helping drive a whitepaper for fifteen hours a week.

Well before the six-month window was up, they extended her contract to a year, raised her hours, and, just like Noel, Sam, and J, her flywheel of accelerated opportunity commenced. As she put it, "What I loved about freelancing was that I had more control over which projects I worked on, who I worked with, and my pay. This enabled me to deliver my best work on challenging projects, with amazing people, thanks to the ability to turn away uninteresting projects or ones in known toxic environments." As full-time employees, we've all had "are you kidding me" moments where you have to say yes to leadership on something you don't want to do. But Liane, once her flywheel commenced, had full control over her work.

One of these potential projects was driving a large, global company to embrace human cloud platforms. At the time, while human cloud platforms were easy to use for startups, only a few enterprises were using them since the infrastructure—people, process, and technology—was lacking or prohibited.

The good news . . . she saw incredible opportunity.

The bad news . . . it had to be a full-time role because, in order to succeed, Liane needed to disrupt existing policies, processes, and internal systems (which we discuss later in the book).

Like me, Liane joined a large company after working as a freelancer. But while you can take Liane out of the human cloud, you can't take the human cloud out of Liane (that was cheesy . . . sorry!). And thank goodness because she faced two enormous challenges, but with the skills she learned freelancing, she knew how to solve them.

The first was that requirements crossed almost every business group—legal, procurement, HR, corporate strategy, and various product groups. Most people would have thrown up their hands at the complexity and intricacy of a large organization, but fortunately, freelancing taught Liane how to navigate various cross-functional decisionmakers. As she said, "Since I didn't have one specialized job like my full-time employee peers, I got really good at spanning across the company, understanding each group's requirements, why they were established in the first place, and how the various groups could collaborate and build off each other's work toward a new shared vision."

The second was that there was no prescribed playbook for her to follow—just the requirements she gathered from various teams. And as we all know, teams have conflicting requirements and varying approaches that stem from age-old policies and processes. For some, this environment spells failure. No bulleted responsibilities. No prior processes to follow. Just ownership and accountability for something no one else knows how to do. For her, this was an opportunity to flex her upskilling muscles. She had no basis of comparison, no biases, no technology she was supposed to use. And freelancing prepped her for this perfectly since she was always reskilling to stay ahead of technology trends, which is a well-documented trait of freelancers compared to their full-time counterparts.

As Liane put it, "A lot of people who haven't freelanced don't do well in chaos. As a full-time employee, someone above you generally decides your fate. The perceived good of this is you have a playbook and bullets to align with. Not in freelance. It was 100 percent my input what I did, which meant I created the bullets and was accountable to the outcomes of those bullets." Thus, instead of asking for bullets, Liane taught herself various technologies within the Microsoft 365 stack, specifically Teams, Power Automate, SharePoint, PowerBI, and Forms and merged the requirements above with these technologies to operationalize an enterprise human cloud program.

The program was a smashing success. Her enterprise went from no processes to over five thousand freelance projects in less than two years. Our industry doesn't have a Super Bowl. But if we did, she'd win MVP.

The deeper insight for us changemakers is that her time working in the human cloud gave her the skills to thrive, whether on her own or within an organization. One of the skills of a freelancer is extreme ownership. As she put it, "You don't just throw sh** over the fence—it's your reputation at stake that impacts your ability to get future gigs." Another is training by doing, or as she puts it, "You don't have those pointless hours for required, but not useful, training."

Whether outside an organization's walls like J, or inside those walls like Liane, organizations are transforming from being fixed physical offices to digital, agile, and project-based. For us changemakers, it's our time to shine.

WHAT IF YOU DON'T JUMP?

Jumping into the human cloud isn't for the faint of heart. Just like counting to three on the diving board, the fear is real. What if it's cold? What if my bathing suit falls off?

But what if you don't?

My colleague didn't, and while he felt safe, he dreaded going into the office because he wanted more time with his kids and was focused on how to maximize his productivity so that he was in the office less. I asked him, "Why even go to the office? Why not bring the office to you? And integrate the office with your kids?" He paused and asked what I meant. Then I asked him, "Why not integrate work into time with your kids? For example, you have a keynote next Thursday. You're going to make flashcards, memorize them, then use them to practice your talk. Why not have your kids quiz you on what's on each flashcard? Then for each you get wrong, you owe them a chocolate chip pancake. Or better yet, make the flashcards with your kids! See who can get more creative." In theory, this could work. In practice, it would not.

Unfortunately, while J can do this, my colleague can't because he's not working in the human cloud. Instead, he's stuck playing the corporate game. And because the corporate game prioritizes obedience over outcomes, while Liane, Sam, and J control what's important to them, my colleague is forced to trade his priorities for his bosses'.

WHAT THIS MEANS FOR YOU

As you can see, working in the human cloud is *not* one size fits all. It's personalized, with you as the driver of customization.

Think of it like soda fountain machines. You can just take one soda. Or you can take some of the Sprite. Mix it with the Coke. Add some Tang. And voila! A masterpiece destined to gross out your mom.

J and Sam are one-soda people—choosing to work only for themselves. Your parents or grandparents were probably one-soda people as well, but their flavor was a career as a full-time employee.

I'm more about mixing every flavor until I find the right combination, and then I stick with this for about two years. I used projects in the human cloud as a springboard to find the right full-time opportunities. I learned a ton. Built street cred. Then I jumped into a full-time role with heightened responsibility. In the future, who knows where I'll be. All that matters is what I build and who I build it with. If that means New Balances and khakis (large organizations) . . . so be it. If that means hoodies and sweatpants (startups) . . . sounds great. Or no pants at all (freelancing) . . . even better!

Meanwhile the hotter Matt (ha), does *not* know what he wants. One day he's mostly Tang. The next, he's mostly Coke. He's the moonlighter, doing projects on the side while having a full-time job. A polite word for him is a "Renaissance Man." The more appropriate description is "professional ADHD." He loves technology. And management. And people. And business. Oh, and writing, music, art. Finding a job that scratches even a few of those itches, let alone all, is next-to-impossible.

Enter moonlighting. Matt's a technology executive, so without a subpoena to get his tax returns, let's just say he does well (especially for the "thrifty" cost of living in suburban small-town Ohio). He moonlights not for money but rather for the chance to at least dampen his insatiable curiosities and passions. He's written code, designed websites, played (briefly) in a band, and, most recently, ghostwrote about technology and management for professionals. Enter Mr. Mottola and the genesis that led to this book.

Instead of a job title or a role, the human cloud is all about delivering outcomes. Whether editing a report, designing a presentation, or setting up a new program, the impact of your outcomes unlocks subsequent opportunities faster than any paper resume.

Ready to start your journey in the human cloud? Don't worry, the next chapter has you covered.

CHEAT SHEET

Lesson 1: The American Dream is at a crossroads. The *old* American Dream—glad-handing and a paper resume—is dead. The *new* American Dream is working in the human cloud, specifically replacing a piece of paper resume with transforming oneself into a digital product.

Lesson 2: Transforming oneself into a product unlocks an accelerated opportunity feedback loop. By joining the Parker Dewey human cloud platform, Noel did in weeks what would take other students months.

Lesson 3: Working in the human cloud works for everyone. From starting in the workforce to jumping back into the workforce, to never leaving the workforce but being there for your kids.

Lesson 4: Working in the office is merging with the human cloud. As the digital technologies powering the human cloud are increasingly adopted in the office, those who thrive working in the human cloud will thrive working in the office as well.

WE DARE YOU

Activity 1: Productize your LinkedIn.

- Step 1: Change everything on your resume to start with a verb. For example, built, generated, drove. You don't take up space, you get sh** done.

- Step 2: Add time-based metrics to each bullet, and focus each metric on solving a problem. For example, increased retention by 33 percent in three months.

- Step 3: Add tangible examples. If you're a designer, do you have design samples? If you're a writer, do you have the exact articles or samples? If you're a management consultant, is there a public research report you pulled from or that your work resulted in?

- Step 4: Add social proof. This comes in any form where others are supporting your work. It could be an article highlighting your work or a recommendation.

- Step 5: Build industry leadership through writing articles, commenting on other people's articles, or reaching out to other industry leaders. *Warning:* You don't have to be a thought leader. The goal is to establish yourself as an expert in your specific niche, *not* have everyone become sick of your self-promoting posts.

Activity 2: Read about the rise of the freelance economy and what it's like to work as a freelancer.

BOOKS WE RECOMMEND

Free Agent Nation: The Future of Working for Yourself by Daniel H. Pink
Gigged: The End of the Job and the Future of Work by Sarah Kessler

5

HOW CHANGEMAKERS ARE THRIVING IN THE HUMAN CLOUD

UNLOCKING OUR NEW PATH
TO OPPORTUNITY

Imagine we're sitting together at Blue Bottle in downtown Palo Alto. (I say this because this is where I am, and this place has a bidet.) You're interested in starting to freelance, but you don't know how your unique situation can work in the human cloud.

In the following steps, you will find a playbook for your situation. It is *not* a magic formula. It will be hard. And each person's journey will be unique. If you're a software developer with a master's in artificial intelligence, it'll be pretty easy (jobs will literally fall in your lap, you lucky ass). If you're a student with no idea what you want to do in life, it'll be pretty hard. And if you're in the middle of this spectrum—say a designer, writer, accountant, project manager, or researcher—it'll take some discipline.

Pour yourself some wine, cuddle up with your golden retriever, and let's crack this!

STEP I:
REALITY CHECK

What do you want? Do you want to be a full-time freelancer for the flexibility? Do you want to do a couple of side projects to meet cool people, learn new skills, and deepen your existing tool kit?

Meet Dave White, a "very typical" combination of artist and accountant (talk about your yin and yang). Based out of Ashburn, Virginia, Dave is a little bit of everything.

Dave started down the typical accounting path—hate your job, but embrace the safety and stability. Or as he put it, "I was going through the system of school and college and society pressures. I thought I was doing what I should be doing. But it just ate away at me, going to offices and doing accounting, and I just really wanted to use my artistic talents more. I just felt so beaten down, like I was going in a direction I didn't want."

Dave didn't swan dive into the human cloud (very accountant of him). He started picking up side jobs as a bookkeeper and flirting with different full-time opportunities. But eventually, he snapped. As he said, "I remember standing there on the phone and having this gut feeling that I couldn't go and do this again. I declined the job that was offered to me with nothing else in sight. I wanted to have the energy to do my art and set my own direction."

He finally took his swan dive on Paro (the finance/accounting platform Sharon used to tell her boss to go fu** himself), Thumbtack (a similar freelance platform), and Etsy (for the artist in him) and hasn't looked back since. With his ten accounting clients, he earns about $73,000 a year. He uses his free time to paint, along with selling funny office art and gifts, including mugs, T-shirts, greeting cards, notebooks, pens, and prints. He told us he receives art orders every day, and one day recently, he opened his laptop to see a company order a thousand art prints ($10,000) to give as corporate gifts.

How cool is that? An accountant who's also an artist? It's beautiful. And it's only possible because Dave asked himself what he wanted from the human cloud. For Dave, accounting in the human cloud provided a stable income, while art in the human cloud gave him his soul. We'll let him take it away: "Besides my children, the other big reason I left my full-time employee job was because I felt like I was pretending to be somebody I'm not. I love having the flexibility to earn income as an artist, which is my natural talent and what I love to do. I also love working with my own accounting clients and being my own boss."

So, that's step one: What do you want from freelance? If an accountant and artist can answer this question, what can possibly stop you?

Here are some typical reasons why people want to freelance:

- Build a full-time independent career that affords flexibility in terms of hours, work location, and variety of work.
- Have a part-time gig where you choose what projects you want to engage in and how often you want to work. This is perfect for those pursuing creative interests, raising kids, supplementing a significant other's full-time income, approaching retirement, or if you are wealthy enough to almost sustain yourself without working (show-off).
- Moonlight to fulfill a desire for passion, purpose, or creative work while holding down a lucrative but mundane full-time career.
- Make ends meet when you're in between jobs, especially in a tough job market.
- Build relevant skills and experience when you're just starting out. This helps build your "life resume" and project portfolio, which helps solve the chicken-and-egg challenge of getting that first job (everyone saying, "we can't hire you until you get some real-world experience").

STEP 2:
GET HYPER-RELEVANT

It is amazing and a little insane just how far hyper-personalization has been baked into our digital world. Whether it's a dating app or freelance platform, algorithms have made finding that needle in a haystack as simple as walking up to it with a super magnet in your hand. The internet rewards you for your weirdness (or uniqueness if we want to use a nice word).

What this means for you is that the days of having a skill define your value are gone. Are you a software developer? Cool! How can you solve my problem of increasing millennial engagement for our product?

This was the problem statement I faced when working with a major financial institution in India. When scanning our human cloud, we found Jacob, a millennial product manager in New Zealand who had deep experience in gamification software applications and building mobile apps in fintech and virtual casinos. He wasn't just a developer; he had hyper-relevant experience—a total slam dunk for the project.

Ten years ago, Jacob would be stuck being an extra in Peter Jackson's next movie. But today, his uniqueness is rewarded by the hyper-relevancy of the algorithms powering the human cloud.

I know what you might be thinking . . . *I'm not that unique*, especially if you're fresh out of school or have been in a rigid corporate setting for the past twenty years. Or, perhaps your parents were suits and expect the same of you. Coming from the East Coast, that expectation really challenged me. I felt the need to conform and be "normal," but I could see the overwhelming benefits of being unique in the human cloud.

HOW TO GET HYPER-RELEVANT

We can't tell you how to be cool socially. It probably has something to do with Instagram, perfecting the right lighting in every picture, and mastering the "people liking you to you liking them" ratio.

But we can tell you how to get cool professionally. Start reading and building. What do you read? What interests you. What do you build? What interests you. What don't you do? Anything you're not intensely curious about.

Getting hyper-relevant will be an intensely internal exercise. It's those touchy-feely questions we all act like we know about ourselves but never actually put thought to. What makes you tick? What are you passionate about? What impact do you want to make? Matt M's favorite: What will people say about you when you're gone? This is tough, and not something most of us were taught in school. But it's vital.

So how can you build hyper-relevant muscle? By aligning your energy in the same direction for a long, long time. Ashlee Vance, author of a biography of Elon Musk, calls this phenomenon the "Unified Field Theory." Because Musk has aligned his energies with technology to enable sustainability—Tesla for sustainable transportation, SolarCity for sustainable energy, Neuralink for sustainable biology—each one of his businesses is connected in the short term and the long term.

For you, this means each project builds off the next. So, instead of aimlessly jumping from project to project, each project trains your hyper-relevancy. This doesn't mean doing the exact same thing over and over. It's okay to have variety. (In fact, it's encouraged.) Rather, you want your experiences to have a common thread or core that you can weave into a compelling story that meets a particular group's needs.

I (Matt C) have worked in drug companies, financial institutions, law firms, government agencies, and healthcare. I have done everything from software development and database administration to project management, leadership, and sales. I've hopped around more than a jackrabbit on speed. I had (or, more appropriately, found, after some soul searching) a coherent thread I pulled through it all—I build and deliver AI tools that help professionals do their job better and faster. That is my hyper-relevant skill.

My secret weapon for this is a very basic Vision Pyramid. If you watch *Silicon Valley*—yes, you can make fun of us for sounding like Jack Barker and his Conjoined Triangles of Success (see Figure 1).

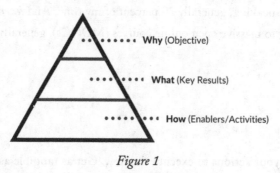

Figure 1

I. Why

Why do you wake up every morning and do what you do? Generally, this is tied to a problem in the world and often to significant events in your life that sparked this as "your" problem to solve. It can be deeply personal. Think about this . . . what are you insatiably curious about? What do you think about when your mind drifts? Or, what could you see yourself working on for ten years or more?

Can you guess what my problem is? I want people to love work. To not say, "Work sucks, then you die."

For me (Matt C), it's equally simple (but took decades to uncover). I want to help people do great things through AI. It started when I received my first computer as a kid and fell in love with the concept of building software that could do something and be useful.

2. What

Then comes your *what*—the strategy and key results needed to achieve your *why*. Do you have a full-time job related to this? Will you take a free course? Will you read two books a month about this? Will you write articles about this? Will you take on freelance projects about this?

We're trying to crystallize what activities start turning into themes. For me, I break it into Do, Teach, and Learn. *Do* is what I'm building, generally 70 percent of my time. *Teach* is something like this book, guest lecturing at Georgia Tech, articles, and speaking, generally 20 percent of my time. And *learn* is everything from reading to massive open online courses (MOOCs), generally 10 percent of my time.

3. How

Now comes your actions to execute the how. Get as tangible as possible. For instance, instead of saying, "I'll read a book a month," say, "I'll read for one hour every night before bed." To get a little corporate buzzwordy, make sure your tactics are SMART—specific, measurable, achievable, relevant, and time-bound.

STEP 3:
DISCOVER WHAT'S POSSIBLE (GOOGLE IT)

Honestly, by the time you read this book, who knows where your freelance projects will come from. We can promise you there will be opportunities. But where do you go to find them?

My freelance projects came from asking the question, "How can I help?" to anyone who would listen (and many who wouldn't). My first client was my baseball hitting coach. Mid-lesson, he told me he was thinking about starting a business. I asked, "How can I help?" and he said, "I don't know, you tell me." I told him I could research competitors and help forecast costs and budgets. Then, for the price of gas and food, I successfully completed my first freelance project—market research and financial analysis. With a recommendation and portfolio project in hand, I continued asking that question, which led me to freelancing throughout college and to this day.

This was my experience, but there are many paths to explore freelancing. Below are three popular options to get started, but no matter which you choose, keep two things in mind:

- You're not trying to find the perfect project. You're trying to find the first project. For this first project, success looks like a glowing recommendation and something tangible to have in your portfolio. It's okay if it is a little (or far) afield of where you want to end up. Experience trumps relevance, assuming you're honing any business or technical skill.
- Apply the lens of "How can I help, who can I help, and where are they hanging out."

Option I

Hop on Google (go grab your smartphone, it's okay—we'll wait), and search "looking for XYZ freelancer," with the XYZ being whatever you think your relevant skill is. If you don't know which skill to search for, try a few different ones you think might be on target. If you're feeling adventurous, try searching for the specific deliverable instead of a skill. For example, you could search for "mobile application" or "design textbook" or "website design" freelancers and get really granular.

Option 2

Search popular freelance platforms, specifically to find the broad platform and the niche platform that fits you. Which is right for you? It depends on your specific skills and interests and whether you wish to be a narrow freelancer honing a specific, highly complex skill or a generalist who dabbles in a variety of related experiences. Generally, the more the platform focuses on a niche set of skills, for example "the platform for finance and accounting," the higher the degree of filtering, meaning the higher the quality check and the longer it will take for you to "get in." But, once you're in, you are competing with a select few instead of the masses.

Option 3

Don't be scared to ask people in person. Remember the slogan "Think global, buy local." For instance, Benek focuses on securing local clients. He lives in Auckland, New Zealand, and most of his clients are located in Auckland too. This approach not only means he faces less competition than he would on the world stage, but it also instills trust by meeting his clients face-to-face at least once. According to Benek: "It's counterintuitive for most people thinking the world is their oyster. Some people believe that freelancing is just doing gigs on Upwork. But there are a thousand other people competing with you. The easiest way to start is to try to be super local and just make as many connections as you can, even starting with friends and family and classmates. There's probably more work there than you realize."

Remember, for the first project, it's about the glowing recommendation and a tangible proof point of your work.

STEP 4:
ALIGN EXPECTATIONS

Want to know a secret? Your client most likely has no idea what they're hiring you for. They know their pain and might have a slight idea for a solution, but relying on them to set the specs, cost, and time frame is like your veterinarian asking your dog how to fix their broken leg. You're the expert, not them.

So, instead of guessing or winging it, put yourself in their shoes, and map out expectations. Most likely, they're worried about (and have to relay to their management) three things:

1. What will you produce?
2. When will they get it?
3. How much will it cost?

This is just the start. They'll probably need visuals or explanations of comparable deliverables. They might need a road map or short project plan. They definitely need requirements for what *you* need. For example, are there brand or design guidelines you're supposed to follow? It would be disastrous if they expect crisp and professional, yet you assume they want fun and sexy. It would suck even more if you found this out at the end of a one-month project because you never shared your work along the way.

Unfortunately, it doesn't end at aligning on quality. We want to make sure your client can't become bridezilla by proactively addressing things like if it's okay for a client to email you at 2:00 a.m. or 7:30 p.m. on the weekend and expect a response within an hour (I wish this were hypothetical). Hell no, but unless clearly stated, why wouldn't it be? Just like driving what you'll do, it's up to you to drive how you'll do it.

Common pitfalls:

- **Communication:** How should you contact the client? Email? Slack?
- **Response Expectations:** When should the client expect you to answer? Within two hours? Or forty-eight hours? Are there certain times or days that you wouldn't like to be contacted or that you won't respond?

- **Questions:** How does the client like to receive questions? All at once? Sporadically?
- **Contingencies:** If you need feedback or a question answered, and the client doesn't provide it, are you still on the hook for the agreed-upon statement of work (SOW)? If the client never answers, are you entitled to the full payment?
- **Feedback:** How many rounds of feedback will you provide? Will you work until the client is happy?
- **Change Orders:** What if the client wants to add to the scope of work?
- **Fu**ups:** What if you fu** up? For example, for a big launch, we had an obvious misspelling. Technically, the contract was closed. Are you still required to fix the spelling? If so, within how much time?
- **Support/Maintenance:** What happens after the contract?

STEP 5:
DELIVER AND BUILD LONG-TERM RELATIONSHIPS

No matter how tech-centric we get, I doubt we'll ever build a world that cuts out relationships. Such a world would neglect the past ten thousand years of human history.

Instead, the human cloud develops deep, fulfilling relationships. And since the machine cloud replaces many of the administrative tasks ancillary to the actual work, operating in the human cloud will increasingly place value on how you mesh what your client wants with what you can deliver.

We trust you know how to build a deep relationship, but here are some unique human cloud hacks to help:

- Automate your calendar booking with a tool like Calendly, and always offer the client to book you through it.
- Imagine you have an hour a week for your client to pay attention to you.
- Meetings:
    Always have an agenda for your client to view prior to the meeting.

Always have questions ready for each meeting.

Always turn on your video.

Stick to the agreed-upon time limit. For an hour meeting, give the client a five-minute warning at fifty-five minutes. If they want to go over, they will, but be proactive about respecting their time.

- Honestly, this is starting to sound like dating advice . . .
- Communication:

Ask how your client best likes to communicate. Could be email. Could be Slack/Trello.

Ask all your questions at once. Not one on Sunday, two on Monday.

Working in the human cloud is only one piece of the puzzle. In the next chapter, we address how to extend beyond our individual biological constraints and tap into the full capability of a global brain.

CHEAT SHEET

Lesson 1: There's no magic formula to be a good freelancer. But these steps will build your foundation.

- Step 1: Reality Check—Why are you freelancing?
- Step 2: Get Hyper-Relevant—What's your hyper-relevant value?
- Step 3: Discover What's Possible—What and where are your free-lance opportunities?
- Step 4: Align Expectations—What will you deliver, when, and how much will it cost?
- Step 5: Deliver and Build Long-Term Relationships—How will you realize the true potential of opportunity?

WE DARE YOU

Activity 1: Pick a website builder and build your personal site. Don't worry . . . your first site won't be your last. I've probably had over thirty site iterations since my first.

The objective is to establish credibility and have one place for people to find you alongside LinkedIn. You're an expert in a specific niche. This site is a short way for people to see that, so use the site as a link when making introductions.

When building the content of the site:

- Step 1: Your *Why* statement—One sentence someone will use to describe you. This should be similar, if not identical, to your LinkedIn headline. (Examples: "Designer focused on Web & Mobile Consumer Goods," "Product Manager focused on E-commerce," "Writer focused on Technology")

- Step 2: Your *What* paragraph—This is similar, if not identical, to your LinkedIn bio. (What do you do? What have you done?)

- Step 3: Proof, also called your *How*—What exactly have you done? This is your portfolio. Use the last chapter's LinkedIn productization advice to build the content of each example in your portfolio.

- Step 4: Get creative. Here are some creative features I've seen on people's personal sites:
   ○ A list of books, articles, YouTube videos, and courses that made an impact on you. Ideally, with your own summary of each book.
   ○ A newsletter.
   ○ A calendaring feature to book time with you.

Activity 2: Create a vision board to make your curiosity tangible. How? Get at least ten magazines and look through them. Rip out pictures of what you want to accomplish in the next year, and glue them to one large sheet of paper. It can be pictures of a strawberry if you want to eat healthy. Or Channing Tatum if you want to look like Channing Tatum. For me, it was pictures of Marina Bay Sands in Singapore, knowing that I wanted to move there. Dream big!

6

WHY TAPPING INTO THE HUMAN CLOUD IS THE NEW CORNER OFFICE

OUR NEW PATH TO IMPACT

Are you reading this to delay the PowerPoint you're supposed to be doing? It's okay, we won't tell your boss. She'll probably find out anyway with the bags under your eyes. But your secret is safe with us. That is, unless you don't want a secret at all.

What if you didn't have to do the PowerPoint? What if you could focus on the content or the strategic thinking that went into the presentation? No offense, but your design skills are like a 7.5. What if you could have help from someone who's as good at design as you are at market sizing?

Today you can. The same way working in the cloud unlocks access to opportunity, tapping into the human cloud enables every single one of us access to a network of experts.

RISE OF THE MOMS!

Don't underestimate moms. Like seriously, don't do it.

Take Lisa, a single mom who freelanced so that she had flexibility when raising her kids. Lisa wasn't freelancing for fun. She had two kids and needed consistent income. So while the freelancers we've learned about so far pick exactly what they want to work on, Lisa couldn't. As she said, "When you don't know if there'll be a paycheck next month, you can't be picky. You say yes to everything."

This created a bigger problem . . . she didn't have the time or skills for every project. When she signed up to host an all-day executive summit, her "say yes, then figure it out later" attitude really bit her in the ass. She received a message from a designer working on the presenters' decks: "The presentations are a mess, the executives keep changing and adding new slides, and I'm at my limit because I don't have the technical chops to have these executives nail down a script."

Her client needed the presenters to adhere to a cohesive narrative, from the messaging to the design. Yet, they were all over the place. And since they were CEOs, neither Lisa nor the designer could go head-to-head with them and say their stories weren't landing.

Fortunately, Lisa had a secret weapon.

Have you seen this meme? "Ladies: What's your makeup routine? I'm looking for a new foundation, preferably liquid but still matte and now that the men have stopped reading we riot at midnight."

Well, this riot came in the form of Avery, a fellow mom, former VP at Ogilvy, and press secretary on Capitol Hill before she started freelancing. Lisa reached out to Avery, and within forty-eight hours, Avery was getting these prima donnas (sorry, CEOs) on-script. Within a week, the presentations were complete.

Because of Avery, the summit went off without a hitch instead of crashing and burning. No flops. No snooze-fests. Just one comprehensive narrative with compelling presentations.

Now, let's say it was you, not Lisa. Do you have an Avery? An expert who can be ready within forty-eight hours? Or are you just looking up, waiting for leadership to tell you what to do next?

THINK LIKE A NETWORK

If you're an executive, you probably have a full-time employee equivalent or "head count" of Avery. Unfortunately, she doesn't actually like you. She doesn't care about your work. She's probably looking at jobs as we speak. But yeah . . . technically, she's yours . . . for now.

But not for long. She will soon realize she's better off working in the human cloud. She'll go work with someone like Lisa. Why? Because people like Lisa understand how the human cloud shifts the power paradigm from ownership to access. She appreciates that it's no longer about owning head count but accessing expertise. As Lisa told us, "I call it the tree of life. The more you say yes, the more you can tap into your network and add value for yourself, the client, and the expert you connected with."

Accessing expertise in the human cloud operates fundamentally differently than the office. While the office has hierarchical org charts, the human cloud has one giant, open, flat network (see Figure 2).

Organization Chart   versus   Human and Machine Cloud

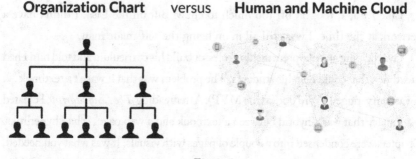

Figure 2

What's the difference?

Here's a hint from an entrepreneur in Elaine Pofeldt's book *The Million-Dollar, One-Person Business*:

> [R]elying on these outside providers creates a more positive, egalitarian relationship than many managers have with their staff. These entrepreneurs see the people who support them as trusted partners, not direct reports whom they have to supervise. They are all part of a community of individuals who are building businesses simultaneously and symbiotically.

Or as Avery puts it, it's like a village, and "psychologically having the village is so key as we see each other as collaborators and not competition. It's an ecosystem, not a hierarchy or race."

Pretty different from the *Game of Thrones* meets *Hunger Games* environment we've all experienced in the office, huh?

But why care about access to a network of experts in the first place? What if you don't need any help? Or what you do is too unique for anyone else?

OUR NEW SUPERPOWER

I miss being able to do it all. Pulling all-nighters. Watching YouTube videos to teach myself. It just seems fundamentally wrong having someone else do anything for me.

Like Lisa, I, too, bit off too much to chew. But unlike Lisa, I didn't have a network at the time. I was still all in on being the self-made man.

I was helping an entrepreneurship professor build his curriculum and told him I had a textbook that could help his students. The problem was that it wasn't a textbook . . . it was a jury-rigged Word doc (a true MVP). After reading *The Lean Startup*, I created a summary that was a hybrid between a textbook and a web page. It had hyperlinks. Chapters were condensed into a couple of pages with visuals. It was what you needed, when you needed it, in a way that stays with you forever. At least that was how I sold it.

The old me would've taught myself to design this. The new me simply didn't have the time. There was a month until the first class, and I was already working full-time at a high-growth startup. Instead of putting my hands up, I turned to what I knew—the human cloud—and posted this job:

> **Designing Interactive Entrepreneurship Textbook**
> **Price:** $1,000 Fixed Price
> **Expected Timeline:** 1 month, final deliverable due 2/1.
> **Description:** We need a designer to take Microsoft Word wireframe and design a cross between eBook and website. The current wireframe is currently using hyperlinks and bookmarks.

Within forty-eight hours, I received this message from Emerson Mendieta-Castro, a designer based out of Nashville, Tennessee:

> Hello Matt! This sounds like a really exciting project, I myself am an entrepreneur so this project is close to home. I've included shots of three recent projects I spearheaded, based on print and interactive design that are similar to this project. Hope we can connect and bring this project to life!—Emerson

I clicked *hire immediately* (no interview). In a week, Emerson delivered the first fifteen pages. I was in tears when I opened the email. He took what I was hoping for and exceeded what I could even conceive . . . from the overall aesthetic to specific visuals and the little details that only a true expert could understand.

Deeper than the specific outcome of the project, Emerson taught me I didn't have to do it all. I could ask for help without being the asshole executive who takes credit and touts his skill in delegation. I created and collaborated instead of delegating and dictating.

OUR NEW MINDSET

Avery is a superhero. Emerson is a superhero. And by tapping into their expertise, you're a superhero with the superpower of unlimited skill and scalability.

Lisa described this superpower as, "There's no such thing as no. Once you tap into your network, the possibilities are unlimited. There's just yes. For every opportunity, I ask myself if I can do it, and if I have the time. And if no, rally the moms!"

You no longer have an excuse to say no. Whether outside your swim lane or not having time, the only factor is if you don't *want* to. You get to choose based on desire, not ability. Do you want to write a book? Or an article? Or create an app? Or a website? Or just a landing page? Or test your product? Or research competing products? Or call competitors as if you were a customer to learn their process? Or interview existing customers and learn what's working and what's not? Wow, those are some seriously diverse tasks, and I've hired for each one.

But the secret is that you have to treat work like the periodic table. Can you memorize every element? Maybe. But *should* you? Ten years ago perhaps. With the internet, hell no. Just Google it. You choose which "elements" you're most interested in (my favorite is palladium—sounds very D&Dish) and master those. Then, rely on your network of experts to fill in the gaps.

The human cloud is your Google for experts. For example, with the textbook, I issued the search "Design an Interactive Entrepreneurship Textbook," and within forty-eight hours, I had the superhero Emerson. And this was before I built my network like Lisa. Once your network is built, working together can literally be easier than setting up dinner plans. With my existing cloud, it's as simple as @mentioning them in the exact document I'm working on. They do the work, respond to the mention with any necessary questions, and when the project is done, I receive a notification, click *pay*, my iPhone scans my face, and the expert is paid. It might sound like science fiction, but it's how this current book was written. One hundred percent digital. One hundred percent virtual.

Do you know that jingle, "Everything you can do, I can do better"? Well, for us, it's, "Everything an office can do, the human cloud can do better."

OUR NEW DREAM

As changemakers, we all want the same thing . . . to make a massive dent in the world. Which unfortunately isn't easy.

Beyond the bureaucratic crap of the office, we have some serious biological shortcomings, mainly sleep and the human brain. Our brain can't know everything, creating a *skill* limitation. And even if yours can (damn you, photographic memory people), you still need sleep, creating a *scale* limitation.

So far, we've shown examples of how to augment our skill limitation. But for Laszlo Nadler, accessing a skill set wasn't enough.

Laszlo started an inspirational planner business out of his home in New Jersey. While he lined up an expert to create the design of the planners, skill alone wasn't enough. He needed a way to scale beyond doing everything himself. He learned this the hard way when he tried to handle the printing of the planners.

He had fourteen high-end laser printers in his home (!!!) but quickly realized over the holidays that "while everyone was celebrating, I was creating my own one-person sweatshop."

Shifting his priorities to locating a reliable supplier, he found an online printing company, and this is when his business really took off. Instead of managing the day-to-day operations, he now focused on growth and asking questions like, "Where will this decision leave us in five years?"

This paid off big-time. Within four years of launching Tools4Wisdom, he was bringing in $2 million a year. But more important than the money, he unlocked a path to insane outcomes. As he put it, "If you can outsource your supply chain, you have almost unlimited scaling available."

Let's be hyper-clear. Laszlo didn't wake up a human cloud magician. He woke up needing to scale and, just like fellow changemakers, couldn't afford fancy consultants or a large head count. This scale dilemma isn't special to Laszlo—we all want to maximize our time and scale our efforts with the valuable time we do have. In fact, I'm sure as you read this you're questioning whether it's worth it (that's a good thing!). But what is special about Laszlo is that instead of the white flag, he experimented with the human cloud to alleviate his scale constraint. It wasn't an overnight success story or a "push button, get scale" solution. As he told us, "It's a constant learning experience. I try something. Sometimes it works. Sometimes it doesn't. For example, as we speak, I'm struggling to outsource my digital marketing. But the human cloud beats the alternative—do nothing—and myself and my business wouldn't be where we are without it."

While Laszlo's persistence is unique, his strategy isn't. As Elaine Pofeldt puts it, "Rather than adopt Henry Ford–era business models, in which scaling up depends on hiring legions of employees, these entrepreneurs choose to travel light. When they need to expand their individual capabilities, they often deliberately turn to contractors or firms that handle billing and other outsourceable functions."

Changemakers rejoice. We don't need twenty-four hours in a day. We just need a little Lisa. A little Laszlo. Combine these two, and we have the changemaker, which is now *you*!

THE NEW EXPONENTIAL YOU

This all sounds great. But let's get real . . . more cooks in the kitchen don't necessarily mean better food. In most cases, it causes more problems than if we just cooked it ourselves. Unless we're cooking only for ourselves, though, that meal won't go far. If we really want to be a changemaker, we need to embrace multiple cooks so that we can drive outcomes at scale.

The office has a standard way to solve this—the org chart. By placing humans into interchangeable blocks within a hierarchy, the org chart prioritizes standardization and consistency. When an Avery quits, there's little to no variation from who's next in line. Pretty transactional, huh?

The human cloud has a different solution—a near-limitless network or tribe of collaborators. The project or task might end. But the relationship doesn't, which creates an environment of continuous iteration, resulting in pretty insane exponential growth in efficiency and effectiveness.

Take my experience last week with Mark. On Monday morning, I learned I had three days to design a keynote deck for a global leadership summit of chief executives at the Ritz-Carlton in San Francisco. When going through a design agency, I'd expect at least a month to turn this around. If hiring a new freelancer, it would be at least a couple of weeks. But I only had three days.

I immediately reached out to Mark, a freelance designer I had worked with multiple times, and he responded, "I'll have a draft for you to review by tomorrow at noon." By 10:00 a.m. the next day, Mark sent over the deck. I made a few tweaks, added feedback, and within a couple more hours, the deck was complete.

It was pure magic. A two-day turnaround for a keynote deck. But Mark and I weren't surprised. We'd been working together for months. With each project, Mark learned what worked and what didn't. So, by the time I was in a pinch, our working relationship was well oiled, leading to exponential efficiency: what would normally take months now took days.

As Mark put it: "I don't think of my relationship with Matt as 'client-freelancer.' We are equal cocreators, each with unique gifts and talents, who are trying to tell a story. And, it's only natural for us because we have invested the time and energy to get to know each other and figure out how to create in a partnership.

What working together feels like now, after these trials and tribulations in the trenches, is that we both come to the table with our own ideas, then figure out how to create the most impact for our audience."

The quote is inspirational, and the results are beyond insane.

We owe the potential of being exponential to the human cloud. It doesn't just enable us access to experts like Avery, Emerson, and Mark. Or unlock unlimited scale for Lazlo. Its final gift is that it takes the friction out of everything not directly value-adding to the work itself so that we can break free from corporate org charts and replace our working relationships with continuous iteration. It enables our tribe's working relationships to create exponential outcomes.

See ya biological limitations. Hello exponential you!

NEXT STEPS

Many of us have our own "wow" moments tapping into the human cloud. I owe my "wow" moment to Emerson. He took an idea about a new type of textbook and made it a reality, which led to one of my most fulfilling opportunities to date—guest lecturing at Georgia Tech. Usually, tapping into the human cloud goes something like, "How in the world do I have access to this expert," finding that person, having a storming period of figuring out how to work together, then ultimately having a friendship blossom. This friendship leads to crashing at an expert's house when you're in town. Meeting an expert's kids. Cooking with an expert. Meeting an expert in an airport.

Matt M meeting the freelancer J in the airport, ironically in front of Hudson Books

At least, that's my experience.

Now, it's time to make your own experience. The next chapter is your playbook for how to do this.

CHEAT SHEET

Lesson 1: We don't have to do it all. We can tap into the human cloud to access expertise (skill) and help (scale) that we don't have or don't have the time for.

Lesson 2: Tapping into the human cloud requires a fundamentally different mindset than an individual contributor or executive. Instead of thinking like an individual contributor, it requires thinking of your work like a periodic table. Could you memorize every element or work detail needed? Sure. But should you? Of course not. Instead of thinking like an executive, it requires shifting your mindset from leading with an org chart to accessing one giant, open, flat network.

WE DARE YOU

Activity 1: Do a workload audit to understand where you can and should augment yourself.

- Step 1: Ask yourself about your current workflow.
  - What can I do but don't want to?
  - What can I do but shouldn't keep doing?
  - What can't I do because I don't have the skills or time?

- Step 2: Imagine you already have an expert waiting on you.
  - If you had an intern, what would you have them help you with?
  - If you had an assistant, what would you have them help you with?
  - If you had an expert designer, what would you have them help you with?
- Step 3: Take a high-level view.
  - Is there a project that you've kept on the shelf?
  - Is there a responsibility you are curious about but haven't raised your hand for?
- Step 4: Keep up with the Joneses (in a healthy way).
  - What does your colleague do that you'd like to?

Activity 2: See what's possible by searching on Google or a human cloud platform for the skills you need. For example, search "front end developer" and see what pops up. I love seeing heads explode when they see the talent available at their fingertips.

Activity 3: Jump right in and hire a freelancer. In the words of Simon Sinek, "Dream big. Start small. But most of all, start."

Activity 4: Read about today's technology helping to unlock the power of doing more with less.

BOOKS WE RECOMMEND

The Million-Dollar, One-Person Business: Make Great Money. Work the Way You Like. Have the Life You Want. by Elaine Pofeldt
Company of One: Why Staying Small Is the Next Big Thing for Business by Paul Jarvis

HOW TO TAP INTO THE HUMAN CLOUD

UNLOCKING IMPACT AT SCALE

Noah: Would you stop thinking about what everyone wants? Stop thinking about what I want, what he wants, what your parents want. What do *you* want? What do you *want*?

Allie: It's not that simple.

Noah: What . . . do . . . you . . . want? God damn it, what do you want?

Did you guess the movie made from Nicholas Sparks's novel *The Notebook*? If you didn't . . . shame, shame, shame. If you did, you've unlocked the foundation to exponential you.

What do you want? Do you want to automate your life? Do you want to be an air traffic controller? Or do you want to augment your skill and scale?

Your human cloud augmentation potential is endless and ever-increasing. It can be as simple as virtual assistant tasks like calendaring, expense reports, finding the lowest prices for things, finding and booking restaurants for client dinners (and dates). Or as powerful as outsourcing entire departments.

For me, augmentation is about prioritizing my most meaningful and value-driving tasks. Take taxes. Could I do them? Sure (in fact, I majored in Accounting). But should I? Probably not since I have no passion whatsoever for the tax code. Meanwhile, my accountant does. Or cleaning—could I? Kind of. Should I? When my hourly rate is higher than the cost for the cleaners, probably not.

Yet thinking at a task level is like buying a car only to listen to the radio, since augmenting individual tasks is not even 1 percent of what's possible. What about creating a $2 million a year business? Or creating the digital rider experience for one of North America's largest motorcycle manufacturers? Or our very biased favorite—creating this book?

Truly exponential outcomes come from forming dream teams. Hyper-relevant. Hyper-skilled. And hyper-personal teams that kick total ass. As Laszlo from Tools4Wisdom told us, "You need a team to accomplish your dream. If your dream does not have a team, it is not big enough."

These teams may be 100 percent freelance. They may be freelancers and full-time employees. The only constant is complexity. And since they're 100 percent virtual and project-based, they amplify the pitfalls in existing leadership and project management. Which is why you have the playbook that follows to drive your own dream team.

STEP I:
DEFINE REQUIREMENTS

What Needs to Happen and When

Imagine you have a ridiculous goal with an even more absurd timeline to hit it. For Matt and me, our goal was to complete this manuscript in six months. Luckily, this wasn't our first rodeo. We've had corporate leadership throw seemingly impossible goals our way and expect a detailed plan within hours. We've had freelance customers asking for plans in minutes. And if they weren't asking, our bank accounts were.

In all cases, what should we do? Take out a napkin and create a workback—a simple checklist of *what* needs to happen and *when*. Start with when that lofty goal needs to be completed, then work back from the final due date to predict what needs to happen and when (see Figure 3).

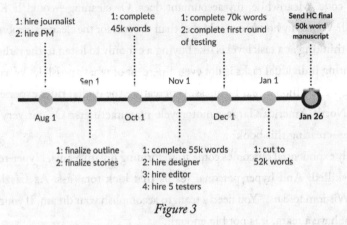

Figure 3

Don't overthink it! It shouldn't take you more than fifteen minutes, tops. Also, each date and what needs to happen isn't concrete; it's really just a guess. The dates will change. What needs to happen will change. But you can't be totally winging it, unless you want a freelancer or team to revolt or you want to be known across the internet as someone horrible to work with.

How Will Things Happen and Who Will Do Them

As you can imagine, a back of the napkin workback won't be enough for scale. You may have a team member on every continent. And while the workback gives you a project-wide view, how will each individual member know what they're supposed to be doing or how they fit into the project as a whole?

We apply the same process for our software products—the OKR framework originally championed by Intel's Andy Grove. Basically, it says, "Let's take this one crazy goal and break it up into the objective, key results, and enablers."

Take our objective of getting a publisher. When we worked with individual freelancers, it was fine. But once we started working with multiple freelancers simultaneously, the lack of one cohesive plan led to work being as random as a drunk stumbling home. Things would get done, but neither the freelancer nor we had any visibility into how that helped us get to the one huge goal—get a publisher.

Here's what we did:

Step 1: Create Objective: The *one* thing we want to accomplish—get a publisher.

Step 2: Create Key Results: The key outcomes that have to happen to reach the objective—an investment brief and meetings.

Step 3: Create Enablers: The activities required to get there—see chart.

Step 4: Identify who does what. See the name next to each enabler in the chart.

OKR for Getting a Traditional Publisher

OBJECTIVE	TRADITIONAL PUBLISHER
Key Results	1: Investment Brief (30 days)
	2: 10 meetings (90 days)
Enablers	1: Investment Brief
	Study 3 comparable briefs to learn best practices and areas where we are uniquely positioned (Us)
	Draft outline of investment brief (Us)
	Draft investment brief (Us)
	Edit author bios (Adam)
	Create market landscape (Lauren)
	Research 25 comparable books and find price, Amazon reviews, publisher, author followers, and areas of weakness (Lauren)
	Create go-to-market (Lauren)
	Create list of potential podcasts (Josh)
	Create list of potential conferences (Alexa)
	SEO audit of current title and potential titles (Dereck)
	Review brief, provide feedback (John)
	Review each section, provide feedback until ready to send (John)
	2: 10 meetings
	Attend industry conferences (John)
	Send brief to publishers (John)
	Schedule meeting with publishers (John)
	Show up, sound smart, follow up with thank-you email (Us)
	Manage relationship (John)

What Are You Hiring For

Hiring seems simple. Just tell someone what to do and off they go. Let's say you have a presentation and need help with design. You hire Marcus, a 4.7-out-of-5-star designer. The night before the presentation, you open up the deck and gulp. It's a Prezi, not Microsoft PowerPoint. The charts aren't designed—they look like a high school project. And the colors aren't consistent with your brand.

You ask Marcus what the hell, and he tells you: "I built to your specifications and price. Your price didn't cover elements. You never specified Microsoft PowerPoint or brand colors. You said you wanted a deck designed, so I designed it to make sure the themes were consistent and modern. Happy to update in a follow-up project."

It's not Marcus's fault. It's kinda not your fault. Rather, the reality is that hiring, and knowing what to hire for, is damn hard. From job titles, descriptions, and requirements to salary, it's hard—like a puzzle with unlimited pieces and no guide.

But hiring doesn't have to be this way. For us, instead of faking like we're the experts, we have the freelancer fill out a statement of work. If you read Chapter 6, this sounds familiar since whether you're a freelancer, or you're hiring a freelancer, a statement of work is that first source of truth.

Here's an example of the statement of work we used to hire our literary agent. We were total newbs, and John the agent was a thirty-year expert. Instead of telling him what we needed to do to get a literary agent, we worked with John to fill out the statement of work template, focused on the outcome we wanted—to land a book publisher.

The Statement of Work We (the Clients) Developed with John

SECTION	OBJECTIVE
High-Level Summary	Get a traditional publisher
High-Level Artifact	Investment brief, delivered as a 40-page-minimum Word document At least 10 intro meetings with publishers
Road Map	Create investment brief 8/20: John will provide template of investment brief 8/25: Client will study 3 comparable briefs to learn best practices and areas where we are uniquely positioned 9/1: Client will draft outline of investment brief 9/5: John will review brief, provide feedback 9/20: Client will draft copy for each section Ongoing: John will review each section, provide feedback until ready to send Ongoing: After each meeting, John will provide feedback based on publisher's reaction, and client will adjust brief Meet with Publishers 11/1: John will schedule at least 2 meetings with publishers 1/1: John will schedule at least 5 meetings with publishers 5/1: John will schedule at least 10 meetings with publishers Ongoing: Client will show up, sound smart, follow up with thank-you email Ongoing: John will manage relationship with publisher from source to close
Comparables	*New Power*, Penguin Random House *Second Machine Age*, W.W. Norton & Company *Rise of the Robots*, Basic Books
Cost	Fixed retainer, % of publisher contract and royalty
Next Steps	9/26: John and client will have hour-long intro meeting, cover a high-level overview of what's needed and any questions from client By 10/1: John will send investment brief By 10/15: Client will provide John draft of investment brief

STEP 2:
SKIP THE INTERVIEW, HIRE MULTIPLE PEOPLE

If you posted a job on a freelance platform, now is when the candidates come flooding in. How will we interview?

We won't. Why spend time interviewing in the traditional sense when you can see how they actually work? When I did interviews, I noticed that I fell for people I found funny. It made for a great interview. But not always a successful project. And then, it was even more awkward when I liked the person but their work wasn't working. Most people are pretty horrible at the traditional interview process, and it leads to bad hires and ultimately letting those people go.

Instead, let the work drive. In most cases, I have multiple people working on the same project. For example, if I need a presentation, I'll have three designers working on the same five slides so that I can judge quality, pick the best (individually or through a combination), and protect against the downside risk of not having a quality product by my deadline.

A really good way to "interview" is to have them do a small test project. If you don't know of a small project, have them build a statement of work. You can pretty quickly tell if someone knows what they're doing based on the quality and rationale of the work being explained. If it looks like something you or your grandmother would write, you probably need to keep looking.

STEP 3:
ONBOARD

The good part of the human cloud—you push a button and start working. An increasing number of freelance platforms handle the paperwork, payroll, and more.

The bad part of the human cloud—you push a button and start working. This can create a multitude of problems that most companies use a six-to-twelve-month onboarding process to solve. For example, here are some very top-of-mind disconnects (yes, this section is very similar to the freelancer's point of view we showed you in Chapter 5):

- **Communication:** How should freelancers contact you? Email? Slack? Are there certain times or days that you don't want to be contacted or when you won't respond?
- **Response Expectations:** Is the freelancer expected to answer within two hours? Or forty-eight hours?
- **Questions:** Can freelancers ask you questions sporadically? Or do you like questions all at once?
- **Contingencies:** If a freelancer needs your feedback or a question answered and you don't provide it, is the freelancer still on the hook?
- **Feedback:** How many rounds of feedback? Does the freelancer have to keep working until you're happy?
- **Change Orders:** What if you want to add to the scope of work?
- **Fu**ups:** What if the freelancer fu**s up? For example, for a big launch, we had an obvious misspelling. Technically, the contract was closed. Is that freelancer still required to fix the spelling? And within how much time?

In each case, the solution is identifying *how* you work together, ideally during the contract phase. Aligning on this prior to the engagement is crucial since you can't just walk down the hall. Add on time zones, the misreading of emotion and intention in text, and you can have a perfect storm of disconnect.

One tool is a master service agreement (MSA). While the Statement of Work outlines what needs to get done and when, the MSA outlines the *how* for the working relationship.

Another tool I've seen for onboarding is providing "handbooks" for the free-lancers, although they're usually more casual, short, and fun.

STEP 4:
MANAGE

Managing teams is hard. Managing virtual teams is chaos. One freelancer is working over the span of a year, while another is working for just a week, and a third literally a single day. As the leader of a 100 percent virtual company with over a thousand employees told me, "We strive for controlled chaos."

Here's a cautionary tale about managing virtual teams at scale. This is an email I received early in my human cloud journey, from a designer I had engaged: "Matt, this is getting really stressful. I'm finding bottlenecks when creating illustrations for visuals that require a high level of understanding of the subject matter. Yet, the only feedback happens sporadically through commenting directly in Google Docs. For me, the rate of accuracy is very low, and I'm spending so much time guessing during the design process and hoping these illustrations accurately depict the copy. Some concepts are clocking in at six or seven iterations before getting it right—a clear problem that is beyond frustrating."

When receiving this email, I was way over my skis because we didn't have the right infrastructure to manage multiple freelancers in parallel. As our lead editor told me at that time: "As the overall editor, it was hard to keep to a schedule. New writers intermittently added content, but I never knew when it was coming or who was writing it for that matter. Juggling multiple clients, and some clients with several projects, I struggled to keep my priorities straight. I couldn't finish editing until everyone else finished their writing."

The solution was leaning heavily into project management tools, both for strategy and execution. There's no magic project management tool. No silver bullet. What's more important is that you answer the following three questions in a completely digital, transparent, and real-time way:

1. *Where* will people communicate? How will they ask questions, see prior questions, and send GIFs to everyone?

2. *Where* will people assign tasks? How will they know when something is due, what is required, and what success looks like?

3. *Where* will they share files? How will they know it isn't duplicate work? (We've all edited version 7 while others are on version 12.) How will they add feedback directly to the file?

For us, we thought about it like a house. Trello was our front door, and G Suite was the interior, ensuring our team operated in a digital, transparent, and real-time way.

Many teams use some combination of Slack or Microsoft Teams for communication, Trello or JIRA for task assignment, and Google or Microsoft productivity tools for coauthoring. But there are many other tools just as good as these. The important point is to have a tool and be consistent in what you use for a specific project.

STEP 5:
EVOLVE

How might we bring our working relationships from good to great? In my case, this meant turning around a presentation not in months but days.

The problem is that we're all pretty unique creatures. What I like is different from what you like. And it's not the freelancer's responsibility to read my mind. But we're also pretty consistent, as much as we don't want to admit it. What we like today, we'll probably like tomorrow. Thus for projects, wouldn't it be great if we could carry over our knowledge and lessons learned about what makes us and our collaborators tick so that each project we start isn't from scratch?

The secret is templatizing everything—your requirements, your communication styles, your feedback styles, even what success looks like.

For requirements, do you have brand guidelines? Or if it's just you, is there a theme you consistently like? Or a particular font? Or certain elements? My freelancers have this prepackaged when they start working on a deck.

For communication, I have a template for emailing specific types of deliverables. Beyond the communication, we've also templatized the actual file format our freelancers work off for product research.

CHEAT SHEET

Lesson 1: Hiring a freelancer can be as simple as texting a friend. But working with one freelancer at a time is like getting a remote-controlled car instead of a real one. Instead, in order to embrace hundred-person teams mixed between freelancers and full-time employees, build your foundation:

- Step 1: Define Requirements
    - What needs to happen and when?
    - How will this happen, and who will do the work?
    - What are you hiring for?
- Step 2: Skip the Interview, Hire Multiple People—Who delivered the best work?
- Step 3: Onboard—How will your freelancers get up to speed with as little effort as possible?
- Step 4: Manage—How will you communicate and collaborate?
- Step 5: Evolve—How will you learn from each project to improve each subsequent project?

WE DARE YOU

Activity 1: Start using a project management tool to track your daily workflow. We used Trello.

Activity 2: Make it easy for freelancers to work with you by documenting and templatizing your work style.

- Step 1: Create a statement of work (SOW).
- Step 2: Create a master service agreement (MSA).

Activity 3: Build your leadership, entrepreneurship, and project management muscles by reading and taking MOOCs from edX, Udacity, or Coursera, just to name a few.

BOOKS WE RECOMMEND

Trillion Dollar Coach: The Leadership Playbook of Silicon Valley's Bill Campbell by Alan Eagle, Eric Schmidt, and Jonathan Rosenberg
The Lean Startup by Eric Ries
Measure What Matters: OKRs—the Simple Idea That Drives 10x Growth by John Doerr

8

WHY ORGANIZATIONS EMBRACE THE HUMAN CLOUD

AN ORGANIZATION'S ENGINE TO CHANGE

> Jacob: Are you the billionaire owner of Apple Computers?
>
> Cal: No.
>
> Jacob: Oh, okay. In that case, you've got no right to wear New Balance sneakers, ever.
>
> —*Crazy, Stupid, Love*

Organizations are in a tough spot.

Unless you're a hot new startup or offer free organic meals and daily massages, you're most likely looked at as a bunch of old people (hence the quote above). Historically, experience has been a strength, but in today's world, it leaves organizations struggling to attract top talent, lagging behind competitor product cycles, and lost in a sea of irrelevance.

What they need is *you*. Not the corporate climber. Definitely not the docile busy bees following the climber. They need you, the changemaker, who will help them embrace a new way of working with the human cloud.

It won't be easy. Politics, bureaucracy, and the old white dudes aren't going down easy. Not until the younger generations refuse to work for them, startups consistently outdo them, and the only thing lower than their retention is innovation. It's their decision: obsolescence or the human cloud.

WHY ORGANIZATIONS SHOULD CARE
ABOUT THE HUMAN CLOUD

Let's start with a super, super basic question. Why does an organization need to care about the human cloud?

Let's return to changemaker Brandon Bright, the software consultant driving a large motorcycle manufacturer in the Midwest (name purposefully withheld) looking to create a digital experience. Although their bikes are beloved, their riders are starting to expect their biking experience to integrate digitally. From building cross-country rides and finding local dealers to running social riding challenges, just a bike and assless chaps are quickly turning into an ancient relic. It's time for a mobile app.

This company always had plenty of options to get stuff done. They could hire full-time (their customer cult following translates into their employee experience). They could hire consultants like McKinsey, Bain, Boston Consulting Group, Accenture, or Deloitte. Or they could bring in temporary workers or staff augmentation through companies like Manpower, Adecco, Robert Half, or Randstad.

So why would they care about a new "fringe" model where people confuse Uber drivers with graphic designers? Because they need to go where the talent is, and it is increasingly moving into the human cloud.

TALENT ISN'T EVENLY DISTRIBUTED

Unfortunately, developers aren't moving to the Midwest, no matter how good the cheese curds.

If a developer is really good, they're hanging with the coconut man in Dolores Park. (Dolores Park is a popular spot in San Francisco. The coconut man can only be understood through experience.) If they're pretty good, they're in New York. And if they're cost-conscious or a bit old-fashioned, they're in Seattle or Austin. Now, this is obviously a gross generalization. But the theme is consistent—there's a shortage of talent for product management, UI/UX design, data science, and the latest development platform if you're not a tech hub or tech company.

So what should we do? Dial in the consultants?

According to Brandon: "Traditional consulting firms are expensive, lack agility, and have considerable talent restraints. Design agencies do not have the end-to-end capabilities for development and deployment. Local dev shops do not have the scale and diversity of skills for a large enterprise. The solution for enterprises if they need scale, agility, and top talent is to foster distributed software networks."

Fortunately, while the talent isn't evenly distributed, opportunity is.

OPPORTUNITY IS EVENLY DISTRIBUTED

As individuals, we understand how to tap into a network of experts. Brandon had a bigger challenge—getting a large company to tap into the human cloud.

Thankfully, the process wasn't that different than for us as individuals. Brandon and the team started by understanding their unique requirements. They knew they needed iOS, Android, Web, Backend, Cloud, and IoT expertise. To access this, they tapped into the Gigster network, which has a network of over a thousand experts and, on average, takes about seven days to connect these experts. (Gigster is a software-dev-focused human cloud platform. Full disclosure: I'm wearing Gigster socks while writing this.)

They then worked with these experts to gain a deeper understanding of what was needed, both in the actual work and the skills required. Within thirty days, they had a spec of the skills, a road map for the project, and a distributed team to begin development.

Some call this the Hollywood model since, to make a movie, everyone—from the actors, to the director, to the stunt doubles, to the set creators—shows up at various times during the project and then leave. Each expert is working on a project-to-project basis, with the ability to work on multiple projects at the same time.

In this project, the "cast" included a product manager, project manager, user interface/experience developer, web and mobile app developers, DevOps engineer, architect, and a quality assurance tester. The team had very specific skills, including Sketch, InVision, React, Node.js, Java, Kotlin, Swift, GCP, and AWS (what movie could possibly have a cast as blockbuster as that?). They were all virtual and spanned multiple countries. And they didn't just show up, write a few lines of code, and clock out. They worked together to crack some crazy hard problems. For example, one of the requirements was a very specific skill in IoT that required mobile Bluetooth connectivity expertise that even the customer's hardware provider struggled to find. Within seven days, Gigster found a developer in Japan who not only had the right skills but suggested a solution that proved later to solve the problem. He was staffed and added to the team within days, helping build custom Bluetooth protocols to connect the hardware to iOS and Android. And it didn't end there—this same expert has been their go-to Bluetooth resource for over a year and on various new initiatives.

The results were mind-blowing for such a traditional, old-fashioned company—frankly, it sounds more like a startup. In the course of a few years, this project evolved from an idea, to a plan, to development, resulting in a mobile app with an estimated 150,000 downloads with a 5-star rating (over 8.8k reviews) at the time of writing this. And customers are loving it beyond the app stores. In one year, the app tracked over a million miles and completed over 25 challenges. Their last challenge had over 4,000 customers.

But bigger than any corporate key performance indicator (KPI) is the impact of the human cloud to distribute opportunity evenly. For talent, you no longer need to live in a San Francisco living room for $1,500/month to get awesome work. (Yes, this was Matt M's situation when living in the Bay.) And for organizations, big tech can no longer steal all the talent. You can access top tech talent anywhere in the world. Yes, you can have your cheese curds and eat them too.

FIFTY SHADES OF BLOCKBUSTER

Thousands of miles west, fancy tech companies stealing talent from traditional industries are facing their own nightmare—startups.

As you can probably tell, I have about as much empathy for large companies as I do for reality TV stars. Yet that tiny, I mean minuscule, slice of empathy I do have comes from what I call their "Fifty Shades of Blockbuster" moment. Large company executives went to bed, thinking they were safe. The college fund was safe. The retirement was safe. Then, overnight, they were inches away from a massive layoff.

What happened?

Size used to matter (grow up!). Now, size is deadly since startups can whip something up in months or weeks that would take companies years, whether it be bringing products to market, updating existing products, or even emerging technologies (so-called greenfield, blue ocean, or horizon three innovations). Then, when startups gain traction, they can use AWS to scale quickly in lockstep with customer demand. eBay, Microsoft, IBM, Oracle. Name any once-flashy technology company, and multiple startups are working hard to turn them into the next Blockbuster.

This size disadvantage becomes glaringly obvious when we look at how startups and large companies bring talent into the "building." The traditional approach within a large company is to go through a lengthy search and onboarding process using vendors approved by the procurement function. When size mattered, a procurement function was a critical advantage, as companies could use their economies of scale to drive down cost. Unfortunately, this creates the conventional wisdom where, when using an approved vendor, you can have two of the following (if that), but never all three (see Figure 4).

Figure 4

Startups, on the other hand, whip out a credit card and head to human cloud platforms like Upwork, Fiverr, and 99designs that all shatter this conventional wisdom.

	LEGACY/PROCUREMENT APPROVED	HUMAN CLOUD
Speed	Greater than twenty-five days	Average two days, but an opportunity to be in minutes if the bench is already built *My record is thirty minutes.
Quality	Generalist, but *great* account management	Hyper-relevant expert, with opportunity for a long-term relationship
Cost	Built-in costs for a physical office, a corporate suite at the local sports stadium, and years of legacy contracts	50–90 percent cost savings Software replaces physical Costs are efficiently allocated since you're hiring the exact expert you need instead of carrying a bunch of generalists learning on your dime.

The impact is obvious. Imagine if it took months for Brandon to bring in and train up generalist developers? How could they possibly keep pace with product updates from all their app integrations? To compete with startups, they needed to embrace the human cloud.

EMPOWERING EMPLOYEES

It's no secret employees aren't happy. When the only thing higher than the divorce rate is the percentage of employees who say they're disengaged at work, there's obviously a massive problem. And while the wise-ass would say "just replace them with the human cloud," the reality is that full-time employment isn't going anywhere. As we learned with Liane, while the traits of the full-time employee might be changing, full-time employment itself remains an effective way to deliver outcomes in certain situations.

But changemakers won't stay in the current soul-sucking employee experience most of us encounter in large companies. One of the solutions for us changemakers is to go off on our own and become full-time freelancers. Another is to go to a startup. People do both to have more responsibility, avoid bureaucracy, and make more of an impact.

Tapping into the human cloud can enable these benefits for those not quite ready to make that leap or those who truly love their company but want to do more. What increases responsibility more than augmenting your skill and scale? What avoids bureaucracy more than not needing your boss, and instead collaborating in horizontal work teams? Enabling full-time employees to tap into the human cloud gives them a recipe for making an impact, which improves engagement.

In the next chapter, we'll learn what's in the way of large companies fully embracing the human cloud, and what some companies are doing to improve the situation.

CHEAT SHEET

Lesson 1: Organizations are facing three massive challenges.

1. There is a shortage of tech talent if you're not in a main hub.
2. Startups can do in months what takes organizations years, with a major reason being that the traditional channels for accessing talent are too slow.
3. The only thing higher than the divorce rate is the percent of employees disengaged at work.

Lesson 2: The solution is tapping into the human cloud just as we as individuals do.

WE DARE YOU

Activity 1: Do a workflow audit with your team just like you did as an individual.

- Step 1: Dissect your team's current workflow.

    ◦ What can your team do but doesn't want to?

    ◦ What can your team do but shouldn't keep doing?

    ◦ What can't your team do because they don't have the skills or time?

- Step 2: Imagine you already have experts waiting on you.

    ◦ If your team had an intern, what would you have them help the team with?

    ◦ If you had an assistant for everyone on the team, what would you have them help team members with?

    ◦ If your team had an expert designer, what could they help with?

    ◦ If your team had an expert data scientist, what could they help with?

- Step 3: Take a high-level view.

    ◦ Is there a project your team has kept on the shelf?

    ◦ Are there tickets your team hasn't gotten to?

- Step 4: Keep up with the Joneses (in a healthy way).

    ◦ What do other teams do that you'd like to replicate?

9

HOW ORGANIZATIONS EMBRACE THE HUMAN CLOUD

HINT . . . IT'S NOT SEXY, BUT IT CAN BE POWERFUL

Imagine for a moment that companies are like your relatives. Startups are like your teenage cousin—headstrong, ready to take on the world, seeing everything in black and white, willing to take risks. They're on a mission and aren't going to let "The Establishment" keep them down.

Then there are the traditional companies. They're like your grandparents—established, entrenched, conservative, seeing things in shades of gray. (I'm talking more than their hair.) They're the ones at Cracker Barrel every Saturday night because they like it and know what to expect. It's safe. Their mission is simple—survive, enjoy life, perhaps help those in the next generation. Risk-taking isn't in their vocabulary.

As a company, embracing the human cloud can be tough, especially for a traditional, entrenched organization. Why? Several hurdles make using the human cloud in a large company risky, compared to the safe tried-and-true path of full-time employees and traditional contractors.

These risks might not matter to startups (hell, they're already taking an existential risk just trying to survive), but for large firms, the risks can be enough to sink careers, shutter divisions, or even bankrupt entire companies. One freelance misstep and a company can be embroiled in lawsuits, lose confidential intellectual property, or stumble into a public relations nightmare.

If you're a company tapping into the human cloud, you need to understand and proactively manage those risks to be effective. If you're working in the human cloud, you must understand why your corporate counterparts may be timid, and you can help put their minds at ease.

A LEGAL NIGHTMARE

If you're working in the human cloud, did you know you're a walking liability to legal departments? Companies may be walking through a minefield to work with you, thanks to the threat of significant lawsuits from violating worker classification laws—the distinction between W-2 full-time employees and 1099 independent contractors.

For Microsoft, worker misclassification resulted in a $97 million settlement from a class-action lawsuit that stated Microsoft classified workers entitled to W-2 employee protections as independent contractors by failing to adhere to guidelines the Internal Revenue Service and other government agencies require: the workers, not the company, have control over the means and manner by which they do their job. Vague? Absolutely. Terrifying? Even more so, as many of these infractions can be much simpler than you think. For example, will freelancers be required to attend meetings? Will they be required to be on-site or attend events? Will they work predominantly on your work, to the point that they do not have the capacity for multiple clients? If the answer is yes to any of these, the company likely needs to hire them as W-2 employees.

Unfortunately, worker misclassification isn't the only land mine. Freelancers also have access to systems, documents, and other sensitive corporate data, but because they come and go more freely, they are not often managed with the same strict controls as full-time employees. No one knows this better than Don, an executive admin who woke up one morning to a *Wall Street Journal* article with the title, "Tech Company Planning to Lay Off 5,000 Employees," followed by an email from HR saying to delete all files on his computer immediately. Don had hired a freelancer to input industry salary averages based on region into a spreadsheet. It was a pretty huge spreadsheet, with numerous tabs, and unknown to Don, one of those tabs exposed plans for an upcoming layoff.

What if Don's spreadsheet also had customer email addresses? This would lead to a potential fine of up to 4 percent of his company's global revenue under the EU's General Data Protection Regulation (GDPR) since email addresses, street addresses, and basically any information that can be used to trace back to a specific individual are considered Personally Identifiable Information (PII).

A CULTURE NIGHTMARE

Unfortunately, legal concerns aren't the only reason the human cloud keeps HR up at night. Companies need to be aware of the perceived risk to full-time employees.

In simple terms, full-time employees are scared sh**less of the human cloud. How could they not be? We've seen how with advances in technology working in the human cloud is becoming harder to distinguish from full-time, butt-in-the-seat employment. When an employee sees a freelancer doing the exact same thing they do, except at one-tenth the cost, you bet they're thinking, "What's keeping me safe from being outsourced entirely?" And with fear and threats come retaliation. They could join a walkout. Or a union. Or leak something to the press. We aren't the safest PR bet for well-established companies looking to pacify their employee base. Even though most companies use what's technically called contingent talent, very few approve anyone to talk about it publicly for this reason.

EMPLOYEES WEREN'T HIRED FOR THIS

Have you seen a job description that lists hiring freelancers as a job responsibility?

Maybe it was hidden under the term *growth mindset*? Or that ever-present, ambiguous "Other tasks as assigned" category? How does a company train managers and employees to engage freelancers when most have little-to-no direct experience with the human cloud? Will the company provide training to tap into the human cloud? Will they create incentives?

Unfortunately, if done wrong, tapping into the human cloud can be even less efficient than just doing the work internally. It can add rework and administrative overhead. And in the worst possible scenario, it can rip away tasks that an employee used to love to do.

NOT ENTERPRISE GRADE

Today's productivity tools really are incredible. There's usually a free version, at least for small groups and limited needs. It's super easy to bring people on. But once you move past teams of fifteen to thirty, it becomes really difficult to ensure privacy, security, and seamless integration. Take the simple activity of onboarding a freelancer. It's great that you can quickly add them to Slack, Trello, and G Suite. But who's accountable if a previous freelancer still has access to one of the tools when something highly confidential is shared? Or if someone forgets to lock down a folder where anyone, including freelancers, can access personal information or sensitive business data, such as salaries or revenue?

Take George, a software development manager who set up his mid-size division using these open-source tools. For the first year, everything was great. Things were accomplished at record speed. Team members, both full-time employees and freelancers around the world, were starting to build great relationships. Then, one day, George goes into his office and is greeted by two HR reps, asking him to give them his badge and his computer and get the fu** out of the building (escorted so that he can't talk to anyone else).

What happened? George forgot to secure a folder from a freelancer when they first started working together. In this folder was a strategy deck of a product that was now out of incubation. A couple of weeks ago, George's team had to let the freelancer go. But instead of going down easy, this freelancer emailed HR a copy of the file and threatened to sue for wrongful termination. Unfortunately for George, that file was considered intellectual property (IP), and the legal department had clear guidelines about not giving a freelancer a file with IP.

This could have all been avoided if these tools had the proper security, privacy, and seamless integration controls.

HOW ORGANIZATIONS ARE
EMBRACING THE HUMAN CLOUD

Given all that red tape, organizations can't just hop on a website and use their credit card to hire freelancers. They need controls for each one of the above risks (and many more).

The current way to do this is by setting up a program, which is an end-to-end process for the company to work with the human cloud compliantly. We could write a book just on a freelance program. Yet for the sake of keeping you focused on driving change, what's important for you are the four main problems a program has to solve:

- Internally communicating about the program
- Enabling communication and collaboration between internal and external parties
- Tracking, analyzing, and communicating data
- Automating manual, repetitive processes

The actual tools and processes used to solve each problem are organization-specific. But the chart below shows the common activities that need solving.

PROBLEM	ACTIVITY
Internally communicating about the program	How will employees get started compliantly, in a way that the org can prove they had a control in place in case an employee leaks PII?
	How will an employee know what they can use the human cloud for?
	How will an employee learn about the program?
	How will the org be able to update employees and/or engage with program members?
Enabling communication and collaboration between internal and external parties	How will employees share files externally?
	How will external parties see only files that fit within compliance requirements?
	How will external parties have access removed when the project is over?
	How will feedback be captured?
	How will communication be controlled? Will there be channels for everyone? For certain parties?

PROBLEM	ACTIVITY
Tracking, analyzing, and communicating data	How will the org know the volume of projects?
	How will the org know the exact projects, specifically the skills they are using?
	How will the org know how much money individuals, teams, and the company are spending?
	How will the org know if individuals or teams have spent too much?
	How will the org know if the program is exceeding KPIs?
	How will the org know where work is getting done?
	How will the org know they are sustainably sourcing (not underpaying)?
Automating manual, repetitive processes	Any if-then logic that can be streamlined and potentially automated should be. For example, if an employee completes a compliance form and their project is within compliance, then an email needs to be sent.

NEXT STEPS

Want to know a secret? No matter what you do, or what your organization does, chances are the human cloud is already in the building. My favorite thing to tell a customer is, "Check the credit card statements." What they find is their employees are already using more than twenty human cloud platforms. And if they're not, well then they have some complacent employees. One of these customers, a large pharmaceutical company, cracked me up when they called one of these employees, asked about the charge, then paused for five seconds. Crickets . . . until they told the employee, "Don't worry, you're not fired, we just want to learn."

And it isn't just working with freelancers. Many employees are freelancing themselves, which provides organizations an interesting opportunity. What if they could combine the good of full-time employment with the good of the human cloud? Jeanne C. Meister and Kevin J. Mulcahy highlight Cisco's Talent Cloud in their book, *The Future Workplace Experience*: "Essentially, the Cisco Talent Cloud combines the flexibility of the freelance marketplace with the structure of a corporate environment. Cisco's innovation is taking the control, autonomy, and flexibility of working in the gig economy and combining it with the structure of the corporate world. It's this combination that creates a compelling employee experience."

Brace yourselves, we'll learn more about the up-and-coming innovations to the human cloud in the next chapter.

CHEAT SHEET

Lesson 1: Embracing the human cloud is very risky. For example, common legal challenges exist like the European Union's General Data Protection Regulation (GDPR), along with common HR challenges like full-time employee sentiment over embracing freelancers.

Lesson 2: One method organizations are using to embrace the human cloud is to set up a program that solves four main problems:

- Internally communicating about the program
- Enabling communication and collaboration between internal and external parties
- Tracking, analyzing, and communicating data
- Automating manual, repetitive processes

WE DARE YOU

Activity 1: Check credit card statements for human cloud platforms.

Activity 2: Organize a power team composed of leaders in procurement, HR, legal, and a product team. The larger the organization, the more they need to not only be involved but take an active role.

Activity 3: Run the workflow audit you did with yourself and your team, except with a different team leader. For example, common low-hanging fruit are marketing teams, specifically presentation design, event brochures, and landing pages.

BOOKS WE RECOMMEND

The Future Workplace Experience by Jeanne C. Meister and Kevin J. Mulcahy

10

WHAT'S ON THE HORIZON FOR THE HUMAN CLOUD

WHAT TO EXPECT GOING FORWARD
FROM THE HUMAN CLOUD

As you can imagine, I get pitched a lot of up-and-coming startups in this space and see lots of problems not yet solved. Below are a couple of these big trends that I expect to see in the next five to ten years. As promised in the beginning of the book, some of these will no longer be relevant by the time you read about them, while others hopefully will have already happened. If they're still available and you want to make an impact in this world, grab a friend and build a company around the idea.

IMPROVING MANAGEMENT

I think it's pretty clear I'm all for ridding the world of bad leadership. Well, what if we could get rid of all that extra stuff that makes us too busy to focus on good management?

According to "The Coach," Silicon Valley legend Bill Campbell, "The primary job of each manager is to help people be more effective in their job and to grow and develop."

Yet let's face it—nobody has time for that. We have too many mundane tasks focused on herding instead of empowering. But what if we could get rid of all this overhead?

According to Devin Fidler of Rethinkery, we can. Using their virtual management system, they built a 124-page research report for a Fortune 50 company by spending a few hours dividing complex work into small tasks, assigning those tasks using multiple freelance software platforms, pressing *play*, then watching what normally took three weeks take only three days.

Crazy, right? Especially since the system handled two dozen freelancers from around the world, and according to Fidler, "We rarely needed to intervene, even to check the quality of individual components of the report as they were submitted, or spend time hiring staff, because QA and HR were also automated by the software."

On the one hand, this is terrifying since a *Harvard Business Review* article highlighting this was titled "Here's How Managers Can Be Replaced by Software." On the other hand, the augmentation potential is liberating for managing beyond mundane tasks.

PORTABLE MERIT

If you're a full-time employee and get laid off, what do you have besides a headline and bullets?

Generic Company, Product Manager,
January 2012–August 2018

Sick . . . you look like every other resume. What about the impact you made, though? Is there a portfolio of designs you made? Or examples of the code you built? Or models? Or what about those interpersonal skills? Was your team better when you were there? Or you made people feel special? Your company's feedback system most likely has that (if you're lucky) . . . why doesn't your resume or however your merit is captured?

Likewise, if you're a freelancer on one platform, what if that platform goes under? Or adjusts their rating algorithm?

Once again, sick.

The problem in both cases is the lack of portability of our merit. In every facet of our life, from the second we're born to the second we croak, we're most likely being measured. In school, it's grades. For the workplace, it's that damn Connect (or whatever your company's version is). Yet why are these so generic and immobile?

Let me Jedi mind trick you. What if a freelance platform intentionally didn't have freelancer ratings and reviews? That'd be ludicrous, right? Well, a couple of months ago, I looked like an idiot when a freelance platform CEO told our leadership they didn't have portfolios or public ratings and reviews for their freelancers. I had backed this platform, and I was sure this ridiculous statement was the end of my credibility. The room went silent for five seconds. Then their CEO said, "Our freelancers won't live here forever. They'll live on LinkedIn, so why wouldn't we want their merit to live there?"

Mindfu** complete. What he exposed was that unless our digital merit is portable, cross-platform, and, wait for it . . . multimodal (I feel like an ass saying that word), the world will never be truly democratized. We're all being pushed to make our merit portable, to have our own "personal brand" (ick). The good news? We'll be better off for it.

IDENTITY MANAGEMENT

Portable merit is sexy. Identity management is practical. To make portable merit actionable, how will we know a person is who they say they are? We all have someone else's Netflix or Hulu account lying around . . . how do we know a freelancer isn't just making different accounts each time they do a crap job? Or, more practical, what if that person's a criminal? Or a sex offender and doing a project for a nonprofit helping sexual assault victims? We currently have background checks, drug tests. How do we ensure a digital equivalent when trusting an IP address over the whites of someone's eyes?

I've been pitched a blockchain startup a week on this concept. But the reality is that the right platform will require working with the real world—law enforcement, public records, government agencies.

INTEGRATING
CAREER GROWTH

The traditional view of success is pretty simple. Partner. The corner office. A divorce.

Yet in the human cloud, it's messier.

For one, the human cloud has democratized and flattened our capability to make an impact. Traditionally, your capability was tied to your title. The higher the title, the more responsibility and resources. Yet today, if you live in the human cloud, you're a director, a CEO, and an associate at the same time.

Second, this world taught me to love outcomes. But how do outcomes translate into career prospects? One of my projects saved seventy-five jobs. One project built the communication and collaboration remote standard operating procedures (SOPs) for a startup. While it felt cool to reference these, what was the tangible impact on my career? Could I be promoted to an "L2"? Or a "64"? At the time, it just meant it was time to find my next project.

Expect both these conditions to converge and for entrepreneurs to build features or models around this convergence. Your skills and outcomes will be quantifiable, and people will know where you stand. Think of it as "leveling up" in that nostalgic role-playing game you love, only in your actual career.

UNCHAINING
THE ENTERPRISE

While building the Microsoft 365 freelance tool kit, I woke up every morning with the same question: How can we unlock spend in the enterprise?

Why? Because the enterprise spend to the human cloud is like the number of riders for ride-sharing apps. The more the enterprise spends, the more money for freelancers, and the more leverage freelancers have.

At the time I'm writing this, the human cloud for enterprises is a monopsony market—a sole or dominant employer that has the power over potential employees. Take a small town where there's one factory. Every morning, the townspeople walk to the factory and wait in line. If the employer wants to pull a fast one . . . well, the employees are sh** out of luck because there's just one factory in town. Yet as the industry starts to grow, some townspeople are able to create a second, then third, then fourth factory. And as the number of factories grows, the per-person power increases. So if factory A pulls a fast one, the worker goes to factory B, or C, or D.

In this analogy, the human cloud for enterprises doesn't have enough factories. There are plenty of freelancers. But not enough enterprises spending to balance the equation. Because of this imbalance, freelancers have little power, and in order to have conversations like benefits and fair wages, there needs to be balance.

The human cloud was initially built for startups that used free open-source tools and a credit card. Meanwhile, an enterprise needs security, integration, and compliance (boring, I know). Thus, expect to see—and if you're an entrepreneur, expect to consider—enterprise-focused solutions and applications.

ORGANIZING
THE HUMAN CLOUD

How will we organize the human cloud? Will we model Ma Bell, a winner-takes-all platform, or will we embrace and protect competition in the form of various human cloud platforms? For instance, will there be agreed-upon standards? The implications are real, far-reaching, and significantly uncertain.

If we embrace winner-takes-all, we can unlock a world of standardization and efficiency but potentially release a race to the bottom. Or if we embrace competition, we can create a world of modern guilds through domain-specific platforms, each one unlocking the creative potential for its members but locking freelancers into stagnation through its complexity and inefficiency.

Right now, we see both. We see one major player, a couple of mid-tier players, and a new guild every day. Each has advantages for the freelancer, customer, and for the platform itself. But to predict a single outcome, with the data available, would be to willingly mislead you. Instead, put the entrepreneur hat on, ask yourself what world you would rather see, and start building.

IN-PRODUCT EXPERIENCE

What if experts lived in every product? For example, your car breaks down, and an expert mechanic pops out of the trunk.

While both will probably never happen (you manually driving, what with all the self-driving technology and ride-sharing apps, and having a mechanic locked in your trunk), experts will live in every software application. For example, in 2018, TurboTax released TurboTax Live—a feature where at the push of a button, a CPA is there to answer your questions. Or just last week, I read an article in *Entrepreneur*, and at the bottom of it, I noticed an ad saying, "Ask an Expert." Imagine if you could push a button and ask me a question right now? Who knows—maybe publishers will take notice.

CHEAT SHEET

Lesson 1: Below are some areas you can expect to see the human cloud prioritize in the coming years.

- Replacing the delegation of management with software.

- Enabling people's merit to be portable, i.e., not living on one platform.

- Ensuring our unique digital profiles are secure and compliant.

- Integrating career growth activities and processes common in full-time employment within a freelance context.

- Reducing friction for large organizations to embrace the human cloud.

- Organizing talent in the human cloud from broadly applicable platforms (horizontally focused) to domain-specific platforms (vertically focused).

- Integrating freelancers within products like TurboTax Live.

WE DARE YOU

Activity 1: Build the business that solves these pain points (we know, it's a tall order).

BOOKS WE RECOMMEND

Trillion Dollar Coach: The Leadership Playbook of Silicon Valley's Bill Campbell by Eric Schmidt, Jonathan Rosenberg, and Alan Eagle

THE
MACHINE
CLOUD

11

RISE OF THE MACHINE CLOUD

TECHNOLOGY—ESPECIALLY AI—HAS BECOME A CRITICAL PIECE OF OUR ABILITY TO DRIVE OUTSIZED CHANGE

Our ability to tap into the vast human cloud of on-demand experts helps us create 10x outcomes. We could have stopped the book there, but you would be missing out on the other side of the change coin, the yin to the yang. The machine cloud is an equally powerful way to enact significant change.

Before diving in, let's define the machine cloud:

> Democratized access to distributed computing power, software tools, and adaptive human-like systems that significantly improve individuals' and organizations' productivity.

The machine cloud combines once disparate capabilities into a seamless, fluid system spanning computational power, software, and data. It brings together the shared computing resources of cloud computing, cloud-native software as a service, and artificial intelligence algorithms into a cohesive whole. And with the exponential drive of technology advancement, tools that once belonged only to the largest corporations can now be accessed and rented by literally anyone, anywhere.

What does this look like in practice? Consider ROSS, a successful IBM Watson-powered legal research AI assistant that is transforming the way attorneys practice law. ROSS currently "works" for departments at law firms alongside dozens of human lawyers. While the computer's work at large law firms helps pay the bills, Andrew Arruda, cofounder and CEO of ROSS, thinks bigger and with a noble, altruistic purpose. He wants ROSS to help lawyers better serve those who cannot otherwise afford legal services.

Ajay Goel, creator of the email productivity tool GMass, saw a need and an early trend toward the use of Gmail in small businesses and increasingly larger companies. He created a marketing distribution tool that plugs right into Gmail so that users no longer need to leave their environment and work in clunky desktop software applications. He capitalized early on the move to cloud software services. Coincidentally, he's also a great example of the human cloud, as he built GMass from the ground up as a 100 percent virtual, remote team of a dozen part-time specialists including designers, marketers, and developers.

In both cases, these innovative entrepreneurs saw early on what is becoming commonplace now: the machine cloud can help each of us work smarter, faster, and better.

WHY NOW

Some see the recent hype around digital, cloud, and AI as just that. Technology has been helping people work for centuries and computers for decades. What is so different now?

A few examples of recent progress will help put things in perspective. Consider the following, which have all happened in my own (still relatively short) lifetime.

Computers the size of your living room now fit in your pocket. The tiny chip in your smartphone is fifty thousand times faster than a large processor for a computer in the 1970s.

Connectivity went from nonexistent, then the screech of a dial-up modem, to 4G, 5G, and fiber-optic. Today's technology is over thirty thousand times faster.

It would take twenty *days* to download an HD movie in the 1990s. Today, you can download it in five *minutes*.

Data follows a similar curve. My original brick of a computer had a 40 MB hard drive in it. Today, my tiny phone stores 128 GB, over three thousand times as much data. With the advent of the internet, social media, video sharing, and now networked sensors (Internet of Things), we have created more data in the last few years than we have in the rest of human history combined.

And then, there's AI. Back in my day (I had to say it at least once!), everything was programmed. The moves of video game characters were predictable because someone wrote them, and once you learned the pattern, you could beat them. Today, sophisticated machine learning algorithms use massive amounts of hardware and data to do what was once thought impossible and have accomplished amazing feats in less than a generation. Facial recognition, speech recognition and translation, Jeopardy, chess, the Asian game Go, and even poker have all fallen at the hands of the machines. The list can (and will) go on and on.

So to you hype-downers out there, this sh** is real. Best buckle your seat belt.

HOW WE WILL BE AFFECTED

Let's start with the obvious. The question no longer is "who will be affected" but "how will we be affected." All our roles, no matter how sophisticated or creative, will be transformed. The extent to which technology impacts our roles depends on how many activities can be learned and, therefore, automated.

I talk to a lot of people about AI. Some are curious, but most are scared. They're afraid that technology will replace them, and for many roles, they may be right. Generally after presentations, the question I am always asked is, "Is my job safe?"

My answer is unequivocally, "No role or job is safe." Automation will permeate into every job, role, and individual task. The grand irony is that roles once thought safe from being shipped overseas or automated by robots are now very much in the firing line. Knowledge workers—from data entry and customer service to doctors and lawyers—are finding their once-privileged roles being at least partially replaced by AI systems.

Automation doesn't necessarily mean that all jobs will be replaced or even that an individual job will be replaced. But what will happen is a bigger proportion of a given worker's tasks will be done by a computer, meaning companies will need less of a particular role. And the overall market will shrink, sometimes considerably. Take, for instance, the legal research software ROSS Intelligence. It offloads the monotonous work of scouring laws, regulations, cases, and agreements so that lawyers can focus instead on how to best represent their clients' interests.

What might have required dozens of humans may only need two today. When that happens, it means good things for the few who excel and the unemployment line for those who don't. So, how can you avoid being on the wrong side of this disruption? Learn to work with the machine cloud.

THE SHIFTING SANDS OF WORK

As we discussed with the human cloud, our jobs are fundamentally shifting beneath our feet. Call it work quicksand. Work is moving from jobs to tasks, focused on solving problems rather than job functions, and while many of us will excel by being specialists, there is also a need for agile generalists able to quickly assemble solutions from various pieces. Take the role of a journalist (still hallowed in my mind). It used to be that they reveled in investigation and research, spending weeks if not months writing impactful, hard-hitting stories. Now? They're on deadline 24/7, lucky if they have more than a day to turn around a story, all while keeping their finger on the pulse of social media. They've been forced to be generalists, dancing their day through a variety of far-flung tasks from research and writing to social media and psychology.

What we do in these jobs is undergoing a fundamental shift thanks to intelligent automation and accelerated by artificial intelligence. AI is the digital/ artificial computation that learns and adapts much like we do. Regarding work, these systems replace every manual task that is *repeatable and predictable*. Office tasks like accounting, finance, shopping, and scheduling are all at risk. Tasks that encompass information-processing and stress standardization, repetition, mitigation of error, and lack of deviance are ripe for automation. These tasks are the "sh** no one wants to do." Unfortunately, what we currently pay people to do consists of 95 percent of these tasks.

Consider the writer. Fortunately for the human, not only is the process complex, but even simple stories require idiosyncratic text: "The Nets upset Motor City's Pistons by 5 points last night in a late 12-point unanswered run. The recent Brooklyn boom and the addition of Cavs alum Kyrie Irving seem to have helped their game."

Consider all the things a computer would have to interpret and understand: (1) A nickname for Detroit is Motor City, (2) What an "unanswered run" means in basketball, (3) That we're even talking about basketball at all, (4) Recent changes in team affiliation, and (5) Local economic development. And then, it would have to form that into a meaningful newsworthy snippet.

Believe it or not, computers are capable of writing such highlights and increasingly are automating much of the human news desk as the demand for speed and continuous updates trump traditional journalism.

So how could a writer possibly compete? While sci-fi and Silicon Valley would make you believe the future will look like Figure 5, in reality it will look like Figure 6.

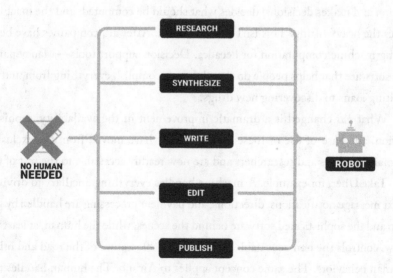

Figure 5

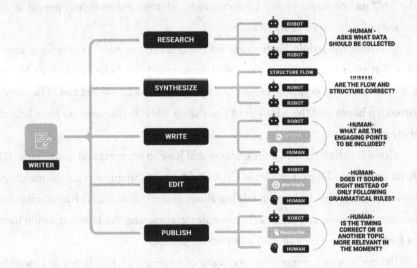

Figure 6

As you see, it's not *all* robot, but rather a symbiosis of human and machine.

In this relationship, a human works with the machine in a clear interplay in which the human's "executive function" (the part of our consciousness that drives action and makes decisions) decides what should be computed, and the machine does the heavy lifting. This isn't a new concept. After all, companies have been using machine computation for decades. Decision support tools—a fancy name for software that helps people do their jobs—accomplish everything from underwriting loans to discovering new drugs.

What *has* changed is a dramatic improvement in the availability, sophistication, and ease-of-use of these systems. They have moved from the exclusive domain of PhDs and researchers and are now readily accessible to the rest of us.

Take Uber, for example. A machine handles everything ancillary to driving. Text message notifications, directions, and payment processing are handled by the app and the sophisticated software behind the scenes, while the human, at least for now, controls the non-repeatable and unpredictable nature of the road and other human behaviors. The same concept applies to Airbnb. The human handles the interaction, but computation handles everything else. Modern planes practically fly themselves, but pilots are still required for the 3 percent of ambiguity current computation cannot yet grasp.

This frees us changemakers to tackle the more important, high-value work. Back to the example of writers. They leverage tools like grammar and spell check, freeing up their time to focus on the high-level structure and whole sentences rather than things like "affect versus effect." The result: we can focus more on expert intelligence and making change while computers do the heavy lifting (see Figure 7).

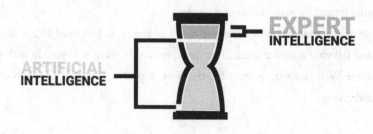

Figure 7

FROM FEAR TO OPPORTUNITY

Once you move past the fear that AI will take over your job, you suddenly see opportunity everywhere for AI to help you *with* your job. The machine cloud is all about augmentation, not replacement.

I've spent most of my career building tools for the very knowledge workers at risk of being made obsolete. These progressive companies and individuals choose to lean into the technology rather than let it steamroll them.

I've helped pharmaceutical researchers find drug candidates for diseases like HIV and cancer in days rather than years.

I've helped lawyers find relevant cases and prior work product so that they could respond to their high-profile clients more quickly.

I've helped policymakers from developing countries find malnutrition programs that worked in similar countries.

I've helped the US Air Force predict which weapons systems would need to be repaired and when so that they could more proactively budget for and complete the work.

I've helped truckers analyze when and where tires fail so that they can identify when a failure is about to happen and safely fix it before a tragedy occurs.

These are not the trailblazing industries you would expect. But there's been a quiet revolution afoot for the past several decades, where forward-thinking leaders from all walks of life are embracing intelligent automation tools. And as AI becomes more prevalent, accessible, and inexpensive, these early trailblazers are being joined by many other companies.

Today, the tools exist to automate many of the tasks you used to use to keep busy and fill your hours at work. The real question is, what will you do with your free time? Will you simply wait for the pink slip? No, you will use it to create outsized change.

CHEAT SHEET

Lesson 1: The machine cloud is democratized access to distributed computing power, software tools, and adaptive human-like systems that significantly improve individuals' and organizations' productivity. In other words, it's the inexpensive application of AI technology to everyday life.

Lesson 2: Artificial Intelligence is here, and it's real. Beneath the hype are real advances and capabilities that would feel magical just a generation ago, all powered by exponential advances in technology.

Lesson 3: The machine cloud impacts everyone. AI will take over an increasing number of straightforward, repetitive tasks. In most cases, it won't replace your job, but it will greatly change how you do your job.

Instead of cranking through widgets, you'll become more of a manager, orchestrator, and conductor for both human and machine contributors.

Lesson 4: For changemakers, the machine cloud is not scary but exciting. It opens the door to creating outsized change.

WE DARE YOU

Activity 1: Read about the history of artificial intelligence and the exponential growth of technology to understand more about how we got here and where we're going.

BOOKS WE RECOMMEND

AI Superpowers: China, Silicon Valley, and the New World Order by Dr. Kai-Fu Lee

The Most Human Human: What Artificial Intelligence Teaches Us About Being Alive by Brian Christian

12

HOW TO WORK IN THE MACHINE CLOUD

YOU DON'T NEED TO BE A DEVELOPER—FOCUS ON MANAGERIAL AND ANALYTICAL SKILLS

By now, you may be thinking, "This is great, but I'm not a geek. I'm not a developer. I have a comparative religious studies degree, for Buddha's sake! How can I possibly hope to live, let alone thrive, in this techno-nightmare?"

Fear not, my friend. This brave new world of humans and machines mixing together is not as scary as it may seem on the surface. The reality is that the skills you need to work with AI are similar to those you need to manage any process or team. The only difference is computers won't talk back, won't complain about their mediocre raise, and won't whine about the lack of variety at the corporate snack bar. So, it's not all bad.

You can't be a total tech-slacker, though. You need to understand the basics of management, technology, and data to be effective in this new world. From there, as with everything in life, you then surround yourself by others to augment your skill set and fill in your blind spots.

Take Cat Casey, Chief Innovation Officer of the e-discovery cloud software company CS DISCO. Cat studied law and has a bachelor's degree in government, not exactly the background you'd expect for someone who spends her days surrounded by technology and technologists. But she found early on that her super-power, her Iron Woman moment, was her ability to combine a deep understanding of a specific subject with how technology can simplify and automate pieces of that work. As she puts it, she "went from being the resident geek in human companies to being the resident human in tech companies."

She sees AI as enabling higher-value work. While AI can be scary, she says, "In the end, it is freeing people to do the type of work they went to law school for vs. the mundane. We're replacing simple, repeatable tasks with high-value tasks. Work will become more dependent on emotional intelligence skills."

With this in mind, let's look at those soft skills that will help you excel as a changemaker.

MANAGER OR KINDERGARTEN TEACHER?

I'm not going to lie. In my weaker moments of management, I have inadvertently referred to my team as children. Now, before you get all judgy on me, consider a few examples from my long tenure as a leader:

- I physically separated two IT professionals who were inches from each other, screaming and ready to throw a punch. (Oh, and this has happened *three* times in my career.)
- An IT professional (incidentally, the same one involved in one of the altercations above) "cut" his finger on a computer fan blade. The little nick that barely bled led to a trip to the emergency room and a week of worker's compensation.
- People twenty years my elder regularly acted like ten-year-olds throwing a tantrum. This was not an isolated person or incident. It's most weeks managing a team of any appreciable size.
- An engineer ran up $10,000 in personal expenses on his corporate credit card and did not pay it for months on end. Umm . . . duh. That's an RGE—Resume-Generating Event—if I've ever heard one.

I mention these examples because in the light of what real management looks like, managing AI does not sound that bad. Yet, I hear people complain about AI not learning quickly enough or making an obvious mistake. They throw up their hands and say they cannot use it. It's weird that we don't do the same thing with our human counterparts. We give them time after time to mend their ways, often hiding or even promoting incompetence rather than dealing with it.

As with managing people, managing AI requires a good deal of patience. It will not get the answer right the first time, maybe not the tenth or even the hundredth time. But, unlike a human, once the system learns the pattern you're attempting to model (or, even better, someone else did all the heavy training for you like Alexa or Siri), it never forgets. And therein lies the true scale and benefit of leveraging AI, especially for repetitive tasks. You are playing the long game, but the payoff can be substantial.

The beauty of this blended human-machine world we find ourselves in is that the techniques we learn for managing systems work equally well for people, and vice versa. Different substrate, but a lot of the same challenges.

So what does managing AI look like in practice? It follows the same growth and leadership curve as training a new team member: train, handhold, then empower.

SITUATIONAL LEADERSHIP AND AI

One of the transformational moments on my path from manager to leader occurred in my mid-thirties when I learned the framework known as situational leadership. I'm not talking about the abstract notional concept that you adapt your leadership style to fit the need. That is true, but the actual framework is more prescriptive and concrete. It maps a person's journey of maturation from high-attitude and low-aptitude, through the "trough of despair" where the honeymoon phase wears off, to someone who has the skills but not the confidence, and finally emerging as a high-performer who is confident in their ability. The goal is to tailor your management style (a combination of encouragement and guidance) to where someone is in their journey.

The mind-blowing concept for me was that this applies not to a *person* but to a *task*. People can be at different levels for various types of work, and your management style must necessarily adapt to accommodate the mini-journeys that each team member experiences. It is a much more nuanced approach and requires more effort (management is a heavy lift, after all), but the rewards are great in terms of output, capability, and maturity.

Working with AI is surprisingly similar. People wrongly assume that if a system is good at X, it must also be good at Y. And they get uber-frustrated when it doesn't work. Think back to your own experience. Have you gotten mad at Alexa or Siri? Even cursed at them? C'mon, raise your hands. I know I have.

How can a system intelligent enough to know that when I say, "Tell Jenn that I'll be home late," process those spoken words into text, extrapolate that I'm talking about my wife, and send a text message, completely fail on an analogous task with an, "I'm sorry, I can't help you with that"?

Like people, AI becomes good at *tasks* through training. And as with people, AI is getting increasingly good at extrapolating and filling in the blanks for *similar* tasks. But we are a long way off from AI being smart enough to be self-directive. It still behaves more like a junior staff member requiring care and feeding than a senior resource you can just tell "go do this."

Let's get back to our situational leadership curve and the process of train, handhold, and empower. For a specific task, the maturation process looks fairly similar.

First, you need to identify the problem. What is the task you are trying to accomplish or the problem you want to solve? Don't underestimate this step. Many an IT or AI project has failed because the problem or business outcome was not identified from the start. Always know what you're trying to accomplish, why, and what the value is.

You then gather the data or at least know where you will get the data to train the system. You don't have to have all this up front, but it is often easier to organize the data beforehand.

Next, you need to actually train the system. This is the most underestimated part of any AI project and another common cause for failure. Depending on the complexity of what you are trying to train, this can take anywhere from a few weeks or months to several years for the most complex systems. Bake in enough time, money, and energy to make it over the hump.

Before claiming success, you need to handhold the AI system. This is the training wheels or beta phase. Identify a friendly audience of testers, closely monitor how the system is behaving, and continue to tweak and improve the system. Frequent communication with your audience and tight supervision of issues and tasks are critical in this phase to sustain engagement and buy-in.

Finally, when you have tuned enough for general availability, it is time to take the training wheels off and empower your new system. Much like people management, a system in this phase can largely run on its own without much intervention or supervision from management. But, also like people management, this is not an excuse to hit the golf course. Set up management and reporting structures so that you continue to track performance, potential issues, and areas for improvement in your AI system.

ORGANIZATIONAL SKILLS

All right, let's get real for a moment. I'm a bit of a fraud. I have built a successful career out of being a straight-arrow, organized executive type who has my sh** in order. And that's mostly true. But it takes a ton of effort for me to maintain this. In reality, on the inside, I'm a free-spirited hippie creative type. I thrive on building things, on ambiguity, on making art (in a weird corporate sense).

I've learned a few key things on this topic as I've grown older (and wiser, grayer, balder, fatter—pick your "er" adjective). First, organizational skills are table stakes for everyone, no matter your background and role. Second only to attitude, your ability to organize and get stuff done is the *differentiator*. Lots of people talk about what they would do—but the successful turn that into focused, efficient action.

The second thing I learned, though, is that most of us aren't naturals at this. I thought I was the fraud, the odd person out. Turns out that beyond your Eagle-Scout-Goody-Two-shoe types who were this way from an early age, the vast majority of us fall into it out of necessity. A little bit of organization goes a long way and is a significant lever for both effectiveness (focusing on the right things) and efficiency (doing those things with minimal effort).

How does that tie back to AI? Much like managing teams of people, whether in a traditional business or this emerging freelance economy, your ability to coordinate, plan, and communicate with AI systems is key in their effectiveness. In some ways, they are still like the dumb computer terminals of the twentieth century. They need direction to be useful.

In practice, this means that you organize your tasks and projects for AI much like you would for any other effort. A machine may do the work, but how you manage that work is pretty much the same. The skills we discussed earlier for working in a virtual, loosely affiliated, agile environment apply here as well. Synergy, baby. I love it!

LOGIC AND REASONING

Gordon Shotwell, like Cat Casey, is a later-in-life technologist. He hails from Canada and, like Cat, was a humanities major in college (Philosophy to be precise) then went to law school. He worked briefly at a large law firm, and while he enjoyed the work, he hated the lifestyle. "It was just brutal," he explained. "I just couldn't see myself doing this the rest of my life."

When he was in law school, he was intrigued by data science and taught himself enough statistical programming to be dangerous as part of a youth crime data project for the province of Nova Scotia. He decided to turn that experience into a career that better fit his lifestyle needs and has since worked remotely at three different technology companies (he's also a poster child for the human cloud, if you couldn't already tell).

What does Gordon do these days? He takes his experience in law and philosophy and applies it to making AI more understandable. "Machine learning has a black box problem," he shared. "I'm working to help people understand what's inside the box."

While he's not a formal statistician, he is stubborn about wanting to know why algorithms behave the way they do, and he's turned this into his specialized niche. "I'm good at explaining things, which I got from law," he elaborated. "My legal clients didn't need to know the details. They just needed to understand the basics and how it affects them. The same is true for machine learning."

The sci-fi future of a robot that understands a human's directions implicitly, with all the context and bias and ambiguity that comes with that, and simply does the task without question or supervision, is still a long way off.

To work effectively with AI, you need to know the basic rules of logic and reasoning, diagnose ambiguity and bias, and challenge results that may fly in the face of such logic. In other words, there's no "idiot-proof" or auto-pilot button for AI just yet.

I'm not talking about formal Greek logic or computer science classes here. Some solid debate skills or frankly a good dose of common sense go a long way. In essence, we're talking about your ability to gut-check the response to test its validity, much the same way you would a human professional.

For example, I may ask Alexa, "I have been feeling nauseous in the mornings. What could I have?" The algorithm might rightly look at my shopping habits with Amazon, see that I have been shopping for toddler toys and training diapers, and may rightly assume that I have a young child and have been thinking about adding another. It naively answers, "You may be pregnant." Unless I'm stuck in a 1980s comedy with Arnold Schwarzenegger and Danny DeVito, I believe she may have it wrong.

This is a silly example but highlights the pitfalls of relying too heavily on AI. Thinking through how and why a system—or human—might come to a particular conclusion lets us not only understand how the algorithm works but also sidesteps more nuanced yet still potentially damaging missteps. When we're using systems to diagnose a patient, park our car, or hire someone, we need to exercise judgment and keep the human (you) in the loop.

ANALYTICAL SKILLS

The root of all AI systems is data. You don't need to be a math whiz or economist to work with the kind of data AI uses, but you should have some basic concepts to interpret, analyze, and synthesize data.

You need an understanding of basic probability. Intelligence is about ambiguity, likelihood, and best guesses. Machine learning algorithms look at how likely a particular outcome is and generally pick the most likely, present a series of options, or synthesize the likely options into a compound response. It is important to understand how probabilities work, and the corresponding "gut check" associated with various probability levels, to know how confident the response is.

You also need to understand a bit about confidence levels. If your AI system predicts you'll earn $10,000 plus or minus $100,000 on your investment, you better understand what that confidence interval means and how likely you are to win big or lose that fancy hipster shirt of yours.

There is a lot of deep theory from statistics and manufacturing quality control, but generally, you just need to understand what is the likely range. Often, this is represented in standard deviations, and a common approach is to show two standard deviations above and below the average prediction. This translates, for instance, in the outcome falling inside the range roughly two-thirds of the time.

The tighter the range for the prediction, the more confident it is (back to that probability piece). For example, an investment outcome of $10,000 plus or minus $5,000 (meaning two-thirds of the time you'll make somewhere between $5,000 and $15,000) is much better than the aforementioned range.

It's also important to have what I call "Excel skills." You need to be able to read a table or chart of figures and understand what story the data is trying to tell. This includes basic calculations and comparisons, an understanding of scale and trends, and how data can be manipulated or biased to tell a particular but incorrect narrative (back to the logic and reasoning piece). We're not talking a crazy accounting level of Excel gymnastics but rather the kinds of spreadsheets you've likely seen from your work, bank account, and so forth.

Why is this important? A lot of data going into and coming out of AI algorithms is quantitative in nature, or it's unstructured content that gets formatted into more structured spreadsheet-like data. Understanding that format is key to speaking the "language" of AI without needing to become a programmer.

BRINGING IT ALL TOGETHER

The skills you need to thrive in the machine cloud are the same as those in the human cloud. It just so happens the "person" on the other end of your collaboration is made of 0s and 1s instead of Ts, Cs, Gs, and As (ahem . . . DNA). Soft skills like management, communication, and analytical skills all play a big part in your success managing systems.

You can't afford to ignore the machine cloud, though. As Cat Casey puts it, "If you want to be relevant, you need to leverage Augmented Intelligence. You cannot ignore it."

CHEAT SHEET

Lesson 1: You don't need to be a developer to succeed in this new everything-technology world. You can learn to work with machines to create outsized impact.

Lesson 2: Managerial skills will help you in both the human and machine clouds. Identify the tasks that can be done well and optimize for those, and plan for or work around areas where the machine (or human) is weaker.

Lesson 3: Planning and organizational skills are still critical, but thankfully a little bit goes a long way.

Lesson 4: While you don't need to be a developer, you do need to understand how a computer (or even a rational person) thinks. Spend some time learning about basic logic, reasoning, and analytics. The effort will be well worth it.

WE DARE YOU

Activity 1: Think about your technical skills. Where would you rate yourself on a scale of 1 (techno-newbie) to 10 (code-whisperer)? Come up with an action plan to move yourself one or two points up the scale: What books, free online courses, or more tech-savvy friends will you use to achieve it?

Activity 2: Research and read more about managerial and analytical skills.

BOOKS WE RECOMMEND

Naked Statistics: Stripping the Dread from the Data by Charles Wheelan
The Signal and the Noise: Why So Many Predictions Fail—but Some Don't
    by Nate Silver
The Situational Leader by Dr. Paul Hersey

13

TAPPING INTO THE MACHINE CLOUD

HOW TO USE AI FREELANCERS TO IMPROVE YOUR PRODUCTIVITY AND GET BACK A DAY A WEEK

We learned earlier how many tasks, both high-level and tactical, can be handled effectively by a network of trusted freelancers. What if you could expand your efficiency even further with an army of AI "freelancers" supplementing your team 24/7, without rest or error? What if I told you that pipe dream is a reality, available to you today?

Look no further than the very pages you read. As Matt M and I were wrapping up our initial draft, he mentioned hiring a few freelancers to go through the text and identify similar passages where we may have inadvertently added the same concept twice (*you* try to keep track of fifty-thousand-plus words).

Well . . . you can't put a problem like that in front of a computer scientist and then just walk away with a casual, "I'll hire a human to do it." The gauntlet was thrown. Challenge accepted. I said, "I can program that. Give me four hours."

· Turns out I was wrong. I finished it in under two hours! One hundred lines of Python code later, I wrote a script that compared paragraphs for similar combinations of terms and reported them back for further inspection. Sixty-eight passages were discovered before any tuning was applied, and the results only improved from there. Needless to say, I was a little . . . um . . . excited. We geeks, well, geek out from time to time. My exact quote to Matt M was as follows:

> Similar paragraph matches 10-10-2019
> @matthewmottola check this sh** OUT!! I added the python script.
> I'm pretty damn pleased with the results, a few false positives or things
> that don't really matter but otherwise spot fu**-ing on.
> Total time to code, test, and review—2 hours. Chance to still geek
> out in an IT exec role—priceless. :-)

Of course, not all of us are programmers. But we can now "hire" algorithms to do this type of work at a fraction of what we would pay for human intellect. The machine cloud adds computer-based "nodes" to our human cloud network of resources, further expanding who and what we can tap into for increased productivity.

WHAT TO AUTOMATE

Before you dive into the deep end of intelligent automation, first you need to find those things that both *can* be automated and that you *should* automate. Let's start with what you can give to the robots.

The best tasks to automate are those that are repetitive, contained, and learnable. In other words, they should be tasks that you could just as easily assign to an eager but somewhat inexperienced administrative assistant. You can't give him everything just yet, but you can give him the tasks that with a bit of training he can accomplish without too many errors or nagging questions.

Repetitive tasks are those that can be accomplished in much the same way, using the same information and techniques to get the same results. It does *not* need to be the exact same steps each time. AI has evolved past such early limitations to better understand nuance and variation. But if you'll only do this task a few times, it's not worth automating it. You're better off just doing it yourself.

Similarly, tasks should be contained, meaning they exist within a problem and information space that is manageable. Again, AI has come a long way. It can work with large amounts of data and produce impressive results. But as we learned before, AI is still in the realm of specialization, not generalization. For instance, a task that schedules calendar events, recommends shows, or even researches the web for a topic are within bounds. The space may be large, but it is *contained*—you can identify and establish boundaries in which algorithms can work.

Finally, the task should obviously be learnable. This goes part and parcel with the first two items. The algorithm must be able to look at past events or groups of information, predict an outcome, and be taught or told the right answer so that it can continue to adjust and improve. Without this "learning function," our computers are relegated to the dumb machine dustbin of history.

Generally speaking, any task that involves predefined inputs and outputs, predictions or groupings of items, information recall, decision making, and language manipulation like translation is fair game.

But what *should* you automate? Before you rush out to buy that shiny new AI object, stop to think about what problems you hope to solve. That will depend on your own personal and team workflows. Understand where you spend a lot of your time. Work diaries are a great way to capture what you actually do during a given week, which often varies quite wildly from what you think you spend your time on. You can also look at your sent email, calendar, and time entry systems to glean common tasks.

If all else fails, a good whiteboarding session can do the trick. I've found that Monday mornings and Friday afternoons work best for getting the brainstorming juices flowing. Once you have your list of common or time-consuming tasks, match those up with what can be readily automated. That's your target list.

We've distilled the most common from our own experience as well as popular tools in the marketplace, which is usually a sign you're on the right track. These are included below, broken out by type of task and with several example tools where appropriate.

Authors' Note: In this book, we include specific vendors and products for purposes of giving you concrete examples and tools to start using. The lists are by no means complete and should not be considered an endorsement (no kickbacks here, we chose dignity over product-placement advertising). Undoubtedly, this list will be obsolete before this book even hits the presses. But the principles and approaches are universal and will be applicable many years from now.

MANAGING CALENDARS

If there is one activity almost universally dreaded by entrepreneurs, freelancers, individual contributors, and managers alike, it is scheduling meetings. Internal, external, formal, informal coffee chats. With today's focus on "productivity" (read, busier than ever) and the corporate masses spending a majority of their day in meetings, finding time for two people even on the same team can be a mess. Add in multiple people, time zones, and loose associations, and you can easily spend hours a week just trying to juggle your schedule. It's about as fun as a glass splinter in your eyelid.

Enter the world of automation. It turns out that scheduling meetings is perfectly suited for delegating to computers since it is repetitive, contained, and learnable. A couple of approaches and types of tools exist in the current marketplace.

First are the simple productivity tools that have a modicum of AI built into them. Calendly, Doodle, and similar products link to your calendar availability and then provide a link and website for people to select times that work for them. The software packages upload those responses and suggest a few times based on the best availability.

Like I said, sometimes the simplest solutions are the best. You don't always need to over-club with AI.

That said, those tools put the onus on those responding and just shift the work from you to them. For higher-level roles or VIPs, you may need a more personal touch. Enter X.ai.

This clever tool also syncs with your calendar, but instead of forcing people to a website to select times, you simply add the X.ai agent to an email address with a request to set up a meeting. Say you receive an email from a sales lead, a potential freelance partner, or even an old friend from school. You just copy X.ai, and it will email those on the thread asking for availability. It works in much the same way as the other tools but has a much more natural feel.

My recommendation, though? Stop first to ask, "Do I really need to meet?" The real productivity boost can come from realizing you don't need to be in every meeting, you don't need to create new ones, and a lot of business can be conducted completely by email, text, or voice mail. Save the meetings for the really important decisions or to help foster a deeper relationship with your network.

RESPONDING TO EMAIL

Next in our hit list of productivity killers: email. Like meetings, consider an alternative first if you can. Email is about the worst communication method for most project-related work. Consider the cognitive steps you must take every time an email comes in. Is this important? Is it urgent? Is it for me? Do I need to respond? What client is this for? What's the context? Are they mad?

You can get lost in email for hours if you let it, and all the while, the real value you can contribute to the world goes out the window. It's like a vacuum for your soul . . . (whoa, deep).

If your organization and team can embrace it, switch to Microsoft Teams, Slack, Trello, or a similar app for regular communication. Set up channels for active projects and groups, and push typical email back-and-forth into there. I know it sounds like a pipe dream, but I worked at a startup where we used Slack almost exclusively. I received about twenty emails a day, mostly from clients. It. Was. Awesome!

But if you're in a corporate role like I am, where email still rules the day, fear not. There is still hope. As before, let's start simple. Microsoft Outlook, Google, Apple Mail, and other email tools allow you to create rules that flag messages, move them to a folder, or delete them entirely, among many other tasks. This works wonders for all sorts of simple workflow needs. For example, you can use a rule to flag certain types of emails that require a specific response (say a customer service issue) with a stock response saved as an email template.

When it comes to actually managing email, all sorts of intelligent automation tools of varying sophistication can help you.

We mentioned Ajay Goel previously, the software entrepreneur who hit it big with his GMass productivity tool for Gmail. He also released a product called Wordzen that brings together executives and editors. He correctly anticipated two trends early in the internet days: that email would become a prolific personal and professional productivity tool, and that Gmail would become the de facto standard for smaller businesses and individuals. He built these tools to easily layer into Gmail so that people with limited technical prowess could still harness automation to simplify tasks like sending marketing emails and using assistants and technology to draft responses.

AI has started to make its way directly into Gmail as well. They introduced a feature that auto-suggests the next few words based on what you are typing. This is a powerful use case for AI and pretty straightforward. Google has literally billions of emails it can mine for common expressions. And, it continues to get better at complex and nuanced topics to the point that even I am impressed. The feature has cut my email response time by roughly 10 to 20 percent—instant productivity boost.

Dictation is also an overlooked but handy feature for responding to emails and texts. I recently picked up a pair of Air Pods (like, three years after they came out—I'm a bit slow on technology adoption for being, well, a technology guy). That, coupled with my iPhone with both work and personal email on it, and I can now respond to emails while driving. It helps me get through my backlog of emails on the drive home so that I can spend more focused time with the kids when I get to my house. #priceless

But can AI help with more? Couldn't it write a full response instead of merely suggesting snippets of text? A number of promising technologies are starting to tackle this space.

Enter the chatbot. The much-maligned early versions, which were just awful, have been replaced by much more sophisticated technologies built on deep learning. They still require a fair amount of training to learn meaningful responses, but they can now learn from the data instead of needing to be hard-coded with narrow questions and answers.

These chatbots, usually powered by one of the big dogs—Amazon AWS, Microsoft Azure, IBM Watson, or Google Cloud—are powering call centers and customer service activities today. For instance, Bank of America has Erica (get it? AmErica?), a virtual personal assistant in their mobile app who responds to natural language texts and helps do everything from access and move money to provide financial advice.

Other more automated approaches like Roboresponse and reply.ai show promise for individuals in a more free-form world than the life of a call center. These are increasingly built into your favorite tools so that you don't need to hop onto a different platform.

MANAGING TRAVEL

One of the most common tasks for many corporate types, at least until seamless telepresence becomes commonplace, is booking and managing travel and handling expense reports. There's no way around it, and the process stinks. It consumes literally hours of an executive's time a week, and with the trend toward fewer administrative assistants, much of this work falls on the individual's lap.

Several companies are working to improve the travel experience. For example, Mezi, which was acquired by American Express, helps manage your flights, hotels, and dining. Hopper is similar and even helps you save significant money by predicting the best time to book a flight or hotel. Pana takes on corporate travel specifically and helps manage incidental travel like job interviews and events.

Google Flights not only helps you search and buy tickets but also predicts delays better than the airlines themselves. Scary good. And Utrip even takes into account your personal preferences and likes from social media to recommend personalized trips.

CONDUCTING RESEARCH

We've already learned that most of us are knowledge workers these days, the pinnacle of twenty-first-century evolution. But our future will depend on how quickly and thoughtfully we can pull together this information using technology. Otherwise, we'll be lapped by younger, more tech-savvy versions of us. Sorry, grandpa. Make way for the future.

Let's start with the most basic of research tasks, the survey. In many cases, we want to poll our colleagues or network for information that we know they have but don't want to go through the hassle of asking each one individually. Simple forms are a good way to go. Many modern platforms offer survey-like functionality, from Microsoft SharePoint forms to Slack and online social media. Products like SurveyMonkey, Zoho, and Mailchimp can take this a bit further and add robust conditional logic.

If your research needs are more far-flung and free-form, numerous automation tools are now at your disposal, even if you ignore the obvious powerhouse AI that backs Google and Bing (for you three people out there). Most content platforms have Application Programming Interfaces (APIs) that developers can leverage, and increasingly, they're cropping up as both open-source and commercial tools that the rest of us can use. For example, newsapi.org aggregates all news events into a single feed that can be searched. The *New York Times* also has a developer portal for accessing its content, both new and historical. And most domain-specific content platforms have their own APIs, too, including higher-education content, science and history archives, and law and government.

Tools also exist that conduct research for specific professions. We discussed ROSS already, which helps lawyers conduct legal research that used to take them hours in painstaking searches and scanning of documents. Scientists also have tools at their disposal from a variety of companies, including Chemical Abstracts and Elsevier, among others. My first foray into the business world was at a software startup that built machine learning for pharmaceutical chemists back in the late 1990s. No school like the old school. But what was cutting edge then is mainstream now, and many companies are bundling AI into their software as a matter of course.

One example of this is Tony Trippe, whose company, Patinformatics, takes the concept of "running with the machines" to a new level. He combines research tools with his own home-grown systems to give scientists detailed reports of areas they are researching or hoping to patent.

When Tony presents his findings to scientists, they are usually blown away by what they didn't know. After all, science, like the internet, is a very large place. "Even technologists can't know everything," he says. "There are certain researchers who feel like they understand what's going on globally because they go to a couple of conferences and subscribe to a couple of journals. But information is growing so quickly and technology is progressing so rapidly that it's impossible for somebody to keep up that way. Organizations like mine help explain the breadth and the depth of what's going on in technology areas."

With the introduction of sophisticated tools in research, I've also seen some pretty impressive—and out-there—examples of intelligent automation. Take the story of David Vishanoff, Associate Professor of Religious Studies at the University of Oklahoma.

Professor Vishanoff's academic research centers on how people relate to others who practice religions that are different from their own. His interest in this field of study began when he was a young boy. The child of Protestant missionaries, he was born in Tunisia, North Africa. He wanted to learn more about those who held different belief systems than his family and felt driven to understand them. "That's been the theme of my scholarship," Vishanoff says. "How do I listen to people better? Part of my moral imperative is to relate to other people. We're awfully bad at listening."

Several years ago, Vishanoff met Dave King, the founder of Exaptive, a software company that focuses on data science. Exaptive finds cross-disciplinary connections within complex data sets, generating unexpected insights for data scientists, researchers, and statisticians.

Vishanoff immediately realized there was great potential to advance his research. He was accustomed to scouring bookstores and buying texts on subjects, such as the interpretation of the Qur'an. But it wasn't possible for a human being to read quickly enough to progress through the massive stacks of relevant books he found.

Exaptive's software allowed Vishanoff to identify surprising connections in his sources. For example, it revealed which medieval thinkers were being called upon to solve contemporary Muslim problems in ways he would not have imagined. It was exciting to see the themes emerging from a sea of text. "I can do the work I've been wanting to do as a scholar all along, and start to see new intellectual currents in how the Qur'an is being interpreted," he says.

"The software is more efficient. I'll know which books are going to be most useful for me right off the bat. I'll also see what interesting issues are coming up that I wouldn't have thought of myself. Now I can research it. I will get more insight about what's going on."

SUMMARIZING INFORMATION

Getting information is one thing. Making it useful is another. Back in my college days, I used to snub the "cheats" who would use CliffsNotes instead of reading the book. I felt like I had to read the entire book to understand the nuances and exact events. What a Goody Two-shoes. And how wrong was I, looking back on it. Sure, in some areas of my life, reading the entire book makes sense. But now that *time* has become my most precious asset, and I dread using it for anything but the most important things, CliffsNotes sound pretty good.

For my consumption of information today, I want the TL;DR version (Too Long; Didn't Read, for you internet newbs). I don't want to sift through three pages of nuanced analysis. I want the punch line, to make a decision, and move on. I cringe now when I receive emails from colleagues that are minor tomes yet fail to get to the point of what needs to be done, who will do it, and when. Communications coaching aside, I need someone or something to summarize my world for me.

AI to the rescue again. Everyone's already familiar with some basic summarization techniques in every search we do. That bit of text underneath the search results title (it's called a "snippet"—pretty cool, huh?) is generated based on your search, what others found useful, and all sorts of other inputs. But automation can help us do so much more.

SMMRY can take an entire document or web page and reduce it to a digestible abstract. Many other similar tools are available. The area is in active development, so expect to see additional tools cropping up in the coming years, including more integrated capabilities from Microsoft Office and Google Chrome.

Other tools can help identify "entities" (people, places, companies) and concepts from documents, which can be useful for quickly deciphering what the content is about, linking out to related content, or even building a "fingerprint" to compare with other documents. One such tool, Open Calais from Thomson Reuters, is used to enrich news content. If you've ever seen an article with a company, its ticker symbol, and a link to its home page, thank a product like Open Calais.

These entity and concept tools can get pretty sophisticated and complex. Some of the tools I've built for companies include deciphering the specific format of a legal case citation and extracting pertinent clauses from a legal agreement.

One of my favorite examples comes from Vin Vomero, founder of Foxy AI. I met Vin while speaking on how to integrate IBM Watson into applications at a Boston meetup. He was a fascinating guy, working to integrate AI into the real estate process. Shortly after we met, he launched this service, which distills home features and associated values based on existing real estate photos. Talk about your job disruption (and I'm not too sad to see real estate agents and appraisers get disrupted a bit).

With Foxy AI, Vin identified a new category he calls visual property intelligence. "We're building computer vision applications to extract information from property photos for use in other applications like property condition scoring. Our deep neural network, house2vec, was trained for two weeks on millions of residential property images. Thanks to that training, our deep neural network has a precise understanding of visual features that correlate with value, and it perceives the gradients in quality that exist among them."

While this sounds almost like science fiction, the approach is rather straightforward with the right AI tools in place. Using deep learning, Foxy AI converts property photos that would previously be considered unstructured data into structured data by turning the pixels into a numerical representation of the objects and features contained within the image. Foxy AI then uses this information to improve the accuracy of existing valuation models. "Those numbers represent objects and features within the image that are correlated with value. We can turn that image into information on the quality and condition of the property."

Valuing real estate is not new, but Vin says Foxy AI is more accurate. "Zillow's estimate is the most widely known valuation model, but they don't account for the quality and condition of the property. We ran some experiments of our own where we collected these estimates from a whole bunch of properties that were up for sale. We predicted the new home value, and then we waited for those properties to sell. Then we compared the sale price with their predicted price with Zillow's estimate. Our predicted price was often closer to the actual sales price, and we continue to improve the solution."

You may not use Foxy AI directly, but if you're in the market buying or selling a house, you may well be consuming the results of the technology without knowing it.

MANAGING COMPLEX TASKS

It's one thing to send calendar appointments or respond to an email. But what about all those other tasks that you do, hopping between applications and contexts to accomplish real-world feats. How can you hope to automate those?

Queue the superhero music. In come products like Zapier, IFTTT, and Coda. io. These applications stitch together various other applications, workflows, and logic to accomplish just about anything your mind can come up with. As these products implement more machine learning into their platforms, the steps will become increasingly easy to discover, recommend, and integrate.

For these tasks, you don't need to be a developer. But you do need a solid understanding of logic and procedure. If you've ever built a decision tree for fun (ahem, me), then you'll be fine. And even if that's not your forte, you can always hire that skill set in the human cloud.

Voice-interactive systems like Alexa, Siri, and Google are also increasingly a platform for automatically stitching together various tasks and sources, letting you reorder common items, and look up flight times, all in a conversational tone. Just remember to say *please* and *thank you*. Your kids are listening.

STAYING HEALTHY

Let's get new-age granola for a moment. All the productivity hacks in the world won't do sh** if you're not healthy enough to enjoy them. The most important question of all is, what will you do with all the free time you make?

Health is a key component to your effectiveness and productivity. This isn't a preach-from-the-pulpit thing. I speak from personal, humble experience. I used to be a big guy. And I mean a *big* guy. Topping out at three hundred pounds kind of big. Eating too much, drinking too much, smoking. Sorry, Mom. Oh, and kids, don't touch the stuff, totally not worth it.

I finally started to see the connection between physical and mental health, as well as my ability to enjoy life. I'd had enough and was able, through lots of hard work, weight programs, and running, to lose a hundred pounds. I'm lighter now than when I was in high school. That's pretty cool.

Also, consider caffeine for a moment. I speak from personal experience here, too. I thought it helped with focus, staying alert, and being productive throughout the day. I was a fiend. Four cups of coffee in the morning, followed by two to three sodas in the afternoon. Every. Day. It didn't feel like a lot then, but looking back on it now, it was pretty stupid.

It took an episode of atrial fibrillation (A-Fib) and a three-day stay in the hospital at a way-too-early age of thirty-seven, right after my youngest was born, to give me the wake-up call I needed. I cut out caffeine, and you know what? The damndest thing happened. I actually became more alert. More productive. Turns out the drug was just that, a drug. A clear mind equals a productive mind.

I mention all this because, in the end, we're talking about productivity. And health is a key component. But you know what's cool? AI can help you here as well.

Weight loss, mindfulness, fitness. You can find a variety of apps today to help you with your goals in each area, and they use a combination of human encouragement, gamification, and AI recommendations to tailor a program to your unique needs and style.

Headspace, one of my favorite apps, uses tailor-made content to help you achieve your meditation goals. For me, it's just about clarity. For my good friend, it's a four-hundred-day meditation streak record. Umm . . . he's competitive. Let's leave it at that.

Other apps, such as Noom and Rally's Real Appeal (incidentally, free for many through their company-paid health insurance), immerse you in making healthy living a habit. Through AI-backed food logging, useful articles, and a live coach, you not only get on track, but you stay on track. One of my favorite AI tool uses is a calorie counter that can estimate calories just by snapping a picture of food—how cool is that? Caloriemama.ai is one such app, and it has a cool name to boot.

A FINAL THOUGHT

You will need to follow your own path. What is important to automate for others may be irrelevant to you. You know you best. What makes you tick. What you value doing yourself, what you would prefer others do for you. Thankfully, while you may be unique, your needs are not. There is enough commonality in the productivity automation space that you will likely find tools that fit your specific needs.

The important point is to find something, anything, that saves you time. The more you save, the more you can redirect that time into making greatness—whether that is in creating something new in our world, learning a new skill, making it to your daughter's soccer game, or just finding time to pause and reflect.

AI is here to stay, and it can take over the most menial of tasks on your plate. It's up to you to make something of the time it frees and not become a casualty of it.

CHEAT SHEET

Lesson 1: Start by deciding what to automate. Focus on the things that are low-value, repetitive, and for which there are existing solutions. It's okay to hang onto some tasks that could be automated if you really enjoy them. Just be purposeful about the decision.

Lesson 2: Start small and simple. Sometimes a basic rule or filter will do the trick instead of investing in expensive solutions.

Lesson 3: Most basic administrative tasks can be automated. They may not be perfect, but remember that humans aren't either, and there is a learning curve for both human and machine intelligence.

Lesson 4: Get healthy. Seriously. It's hard to be a changemaker when you're out of energy, incapacitated, or worse.

WE DARE YOU

Activity 1: Write down a list of tasks you do regularly in your day-to-day life, relating to work, projects, personal, or whatever. Rank them in terms of the level of effort, i.e., which ones will give you the most time back.

Activity 2: Research solutions for the top five items, including those mentioned in this chapter. Pick at least two of them to implement in the next month.

Activity 3: Read about how others have leveraged the machine cloud to their advantage.

BOOKS WE RECOMMEND

Predictive Analytics: The Power to Predict Who Will Click, Buy, Lie, or Die by Eric Siegel

14

UNLOCKING THE MACHINE CLOUD IN ORGANIZATIONS

HOW YOUR COMPANY CAN USE AI TOOLS TO SUPERCHARGE YOUR BUSINESS

Whether you fly solo or are part of a company, the machine cloud can dramatically increase your scale and make you a productivity rock star. But if we stopped there, we'd miss out on an even bigger exponential boost: AI in organizations.

It's one thing to boost an individual's productivity. But much like the combinatorial power of aligning people on a common purpose, the growth is even more pronounced when you pair those people with automation technology. It's like an army of cyborgs ready to take on the world (in a good way, of course).

It's easier said than done, though. I often hear people say that intelligent automation won't work for them. Their company is too large and bureaucratic to get anything through the bigwig gatekeepers. They're too small and can't afford expensive software. They're not technical enough to use the tools. They're too technical, and the tools aren't sophisticated enough. The list of excuses (sorry, I'm calling it like I see it) goes on and on.

The reality is that you can be successful no matter what your situation. Technology has advanced to the point that these tools are approachable and affordable for all walks of life.

Consider how AI can help teams from one to one hundred thousand.

FREELANCERS AND SMALL BUSINESSES

As we talked about previously, for you armies of one out there, intelligent automation tools help scale yourself and your one-person business. How nice would it be to have your executive assistant accessible whenever and wherever you are. Need to schedule that meeting? Done. Need a reservation for you and your client at that hip new restaurant downtown? Already booked and added to your calendar. Pay bills, conduct research, write a pitch deck. Done, done, done.

Increasingly, tools can help you with day-to-day tasks that, while trivial in isolation, add up to real hours lost and potentially saved. Elaine Pofeldt discusses the importance of optimizing and automating tasks in her book, *The Million-Dollar, One-Person Business*. Elaine used these techniques to scale her own business and shares tips for others going out on that scary limb known as a sole proprietorship. She shares that you do not need to be overly technical. These tools are approachable for the average computer-literate person.

Many of the tools that one-person companies and small businesses use—accounting and tax software, payroll, marketing and email campaign systems, website builders, domain-specific applications from software development to building design—are now incorporating AI right into their platforms. You reap the benefits of the big-dollar investments they make, while the cost is spread across their millions of users.

Take Salesforce, for example, the juggernaut in the customer relationship management space, which has a healthy small business footprint. They introduced an AI chatbot and assistant called Einstein that is increasingly integrated into their various offerings (seriously, I have no idea how they got away with using that name).

If you work for a nonprofit (bless your heart), these tools are surprisingly in reach for you as well. Many of the software applications available to small businesses have nonprofit discounts that make it affordable for those on tight budgets. I was on the board of a local healthcare nonprofit for several years, which bootstrapped their way from a scrappy group of volunteers to a multimillion-dollar operation using mostly free and heavily discounted licenses for software like Salesforce, Microsoft Office, and Dropbox, all of which have pretty robust automation capabilities out of the box.

INDIVIDUALS AND TEAMS IN LARGE COMPANIES

So you work at a larger company? A cog in the proverbial wheel of industry? Alas, such tools are out of your reach. Right? Wrong. At least not anymore.

Much to the IT department's dismay, "shadow IT" has invaded corporate America (and beyond) in a significant way. Shadow IT is the term for when a group outside of the technology department researches, selects, uses, and even pays for software.

Historically, IT controlled the purse strings and security settings on the desktop, which was great for them and their ability to centrally manage the environment, but it tended to stifle innovation and individuality. With the advent of software as a service (SaaS), many productivity tools can now be purchased by a manager or business group directly, without IT's involvement or even awareness. And the software tends to be lightweight or browser-based—so IT is not needed to install the software.

Many enterprise productivity tools start as a "freemium" trial in a few teams within an organization. And then, they grow virally until IT is forced to bless the application. Dropbox, Lucidchart, Slack, Smartsheet—these productivity tools all work similarly.

If you have a desire to use tools for personal or team productivity, chances are you can find a way to do so for free or paid for by the company. Worst case, most of these tools are cheap enough that it's worth paying for it out-of-pocket just for the lack of headaches and immediate productivity boost.

ENTERPRISE CAPABILITIES IN LARGE COMPANIES

The above approach works fine for smaller, largely isolated tools. But for many of the heavy-hitting intelligent automation platforms and enterprise software that can truly transform an entire line of business, you're going to need much more support and acceptance. Enter the intrapreneur, the "insider" changemaker.

Like their non-corporate counterparts, the intrapreneur is someone with a passion for building something new, for disrupting the status quo, and for creating new value in the world. They just choose to do so within the four walls of an established company rather than going all in on a new venture. Often, their family situation does not offer them the opportunity to quit their job, skip salary for a year, and eat ramen noodles on the floor of a studio apartment. But in other ways, they're just as passionate about being a change agent.

If you have an idea for introducing some serious AI capabilities in your organization, you either need to be an intrapreneur or find one fast. With how new—in the eyes of an entrenched organization—and untested some of these platforms are, you'll need a champion to drive this change through the inevitable challenges that sideline so many projects. But the effort can be worth it, often with 10x, 100x, or even 1,000x gains in productivity.

What kinds of tools fit this bill? They tend to fall into a few general buckets.

First, and potentially the most lucrative but also most risky from a business perspective, is a whole new product offering driven primarily by AI. This is where you are selling the actual capability, tailored to your customers and industry. You could package up the institutional knowledge of your professionals, wrap an AI chatbot front-end to it, and sell access at a much-discounted cost compared to your professionals' typical hourly rate. Or you could create a service that automatically tags and classifies content, corrects red-eye in photos, provides virtual companionship for autistic children—the list goes on and on. The point is, the intelligent automation *is* the business, and the business rises and falls on AI's success.

Second, more common and less risky, is introducing AI into an existing product or service. The chatbot on your travel website, the virtual fashion consultant helping match your wardrobe, and the medical software that gives you expert machine-assisted diagnoses all fit that bill. In essence, you already have a thriving service, and you invest some of that hard-earned profit to make the service even more valuable or scale more efficiently.

Finally, you can make a real impact in the less sexy but still important area of operations. In the world of finance, this impacts the bottom line (costs and margin) instead of the top line (revenue). You can still improve the health and financial vitality of the company, while improving the quality of life for employees, by automating mundane parts of jobs like billing, project and task management, repetitive questions to customer service, and the like.

In my current role, I run technology for an IT services company. I was hired in part to help streamline and automate the entirely unsexy business of data center infrastructure. Our company provides a service similar to Amazon's AWS, which is heavily automated, but we were still doing things in a very manual, archaic way. Over the past several years, I've worked with the team to transform the way we deploy hardware and platforms. The result? We've been able to keep head count steady while growing our business 300 percent.

The dark side of improving operations and the bottom line is that cost savings often come by way of people's jobs. My hope is that companies grow their way out of this problem (doing more with less and not having to hire as many people, as we did). But for stagnating and shrinking companies, often the only way to improve financial performance is to cut costs. And what is one of the most expensive parts of any business? Salaries.

The best way I've found to avoid this rolling tide is to become part of the solution instead of waiting for the water to pull you under. Often, if you're helping make something positive happen, there's a good role waiting for you on the other side (at that company or another that sees value in what you've accomplished).

LEADERS IN LARGE COMPANIES

For you executive types, you're likely not using these tools daily, although you well could and would benefit from it. Instead, you're making the decisions that drive which initiatives are prioritized, which technologies are implemented, and how you assess their success. What you decide, and how effective you are in doing so, impacts entire lines of business and hundreds or even thousands of lives. No pressure, right?

AI can be both the helper and the solution.

In terms of assisting you in this Herculean effort, intelligent automation tools exist to help with analysis and prioritization of initiatives. Portfolio management tools, financial models, automated marketing validation like A/B testing, and even more sophisticated tools like simulation modeling all contribute to better-informed decisions.

You may have heard of the phrase "data-driven culture" or "data-driven organization," which refers to the practice of using information to guide decisions rather than hunches and intuition. This extends to the machine cloud as well. We're not just trusting data to lead the way, but we're now trusting software that digests and interprets that data to give us insight and to do so in an unbiased way. We're fast approaching the era of the AI-driven organization.

As an executive, you also have a significant and direct impact on where and how you bring AI into your business. It is your responsibility to prioritize intelligent automation in your business strategy, product road maps, and key initiatives. Without your direct support, any attempts to introduce the technology will be fighting an uphill battle. But top-down sponsorship isn't enough. You also need to drive and foster the organizational change—priorities, culture, habits—necessary to sustain such a transformation to everyone from your management team to the frontline workers.

This transformation is imperative for all companies, no matter your size and station in life. It may be viewed as a nice-to-have and competitive advantage now, but it will be a must-have and competitive imperative tomorrow, given what's coming in the machine cloud. Let's take a look at what's on the horizon.

CHEAT SHEET

Lesson 1: The machine cloud is equally effective for individuals, small companies, and large enterprises, but the techniques change.

Lesson 2: Even within a company, you can use AI tools to be much more effective at your job, in much the same way as if you were flying solo.

Lesson 3: Bringing AI into an organization more broadly is still fairly hard, as it is viewed as new, untrustworthy, threatening, and expensive.

But you are a changemaker, an intrapreneur, and you can use the tools of change to build buy-in and adoption.

Lesson 4: If you lead an organization, ensure that your strategy and road map are on the right side of the machine cloud. Determine how AI technology can help you stay ahead of your competitors rather than left in the dust.

WE DARE YOU

Activity 1: If you are currently within a company (if not, live vicariously through a friend), consider your organization's attitude toward AI and technology in general. Are they skeptical? Downright hostile? Cautiously optimistic? Guns blazing with innovation?

Activity 2: How can you help advance the organization's current attitude? Come up with two tangible actions you can take to improve the situation. A few suggestions: give a lunch-and-learn on how AI has helped your industry, do a small internal pilot and show beneficial results, or write and publish an article.

Activity 3: Survey which products are in your space today that either are AI-based or have AI built into key functions (e.g., Salesforce). Share what you find with your team and boss.

Activity 4: Read more about the machine cloud in organizations.

BOOKS WE RECOMMEND

The Algorithmic Leader: How to Be Smart When Machines Are Smarter Than You by Mike Walsh
Applied Artificial Intelligence: A Handbook for Business Leaders by Mariya Yao, Adelyn Zhou, and Marlene Jia
Artificial Intelligence and Machine Learning for Business by Scott Chesterton

15

WHAT'S ON THE HORIZON

AI WILL BECOME MORE PERVASIVE, GENERALIZABLE, AND PERSONALIZED

Imagine for a moment the potential world of tomorrow. You stroll into the office at 9:30 a.m. (after all, productivity is about output now, not when and how you punch the clock). Instead of badging through security, you simply walk through an AI-enabled facial recognition system that recognizes you and your company. It knows which hoteling office you'll occupy today and already has the lights on, your digital pictures loaded on the frame on your desk, and your virtual touch-based desktop ready to go when you arrive.

You fire up your morning project task board and see that you have a few overdue tasks, a project that is yellow and requires attention, and a couple of urgent messages from your global virtual team.

You tackle the first morning rush before settling into your project work for the day. You're creating some documents: a pitch deck, a contract, a blog post to be promoted by marketing. Your AI assistant has already pulled together drafts for you to review and augment as you see appropriate. It's saved you and your team hours of work.

A former work colleague is in town and pings you for lunch. Your AI assistant confirms you have time and asks if you'd like to meet her. You say yes, and it takes care of the rest of the logistics. It knows you love sushi, as does your friend based on her social media feed, and makes a reservation online. In the meantime, your handy AI assistant lets you know she's launching a new product line and just posted a freelance role for design work.

You get back from lunch to find several design proofs for one of your clients' brand launch. You review and make adjustments to the one you like best before sending it on. Your AI assistant already posted several articles to social media and alerts you that one of your prospective clients just liked and commented on one in particular. It automatically creates a relevant message to your prospect, thanking them and asking if they'd like to meet and chat on the topic further.

Your commute has improved significantly in the last few years. Sure, you still need to make your way out of the city, but congestion is better thanks to AI-optimized traffic lights and public transportation. You use the microphone embedded in your cheek to walk through a variety of tasks with your AI assistant, which dutifully starts churning through the data. Responses to your tasks will be waiting for you when you get home. You tear through those additional tasks before calling it quits for the day. After all, you're off to meet a date that your AI assistant swears is your soul mate. C'est la vie!

Authors' Note: Okay, I had fun writing this. A bit hokey for sure, but I'm a geek-romantic. If it feels like the end of Spaceship Earth at Epcot, where it creates the "You of Tomorrow," that's exactly what I was going for. It's a fine line between futuristic and kitschy. I surf that razor's edge.

All kidding aside, this future is not as far off as you might think. Much of the underlying technology that will make this vision a reality already exists. The barriers of entry for AI to become more pervasive are already being lowered. And increasingly, we live in an interconnected virtual world that makes stitching together disparate pieces of information easier.

EVERYDAY AI

When I started building decision support software in the early 2000s, we "rolled our own" algorithms for just about everything. Available commercial tools were limited, expensive, and often were not scalable or flexible enough to meet our needs. The result? It took a lot of time and money to build capabilities, and the barrier to entry was very steep. Only the largest organizations and most expensive use cases, i.e., drug discovery, warranted the investment.

As a case in point, I built a document search and analytics product in the mid-2000s that took eighteen months, a team of five developers, and a total budget of $1.5 million. Fast-forward to a few years ago when I built an almost identical product for a different use case and industry. I used open-source and free-for-commercial-use software, built the tool by myself, and had it to market in three months—at a grand total of just $50,000 in all. My, how times have changed.

Today's AI software, while far more common and shrink-wrapped thanks to titans like Microsoft, Google, Amazon, and IBM, is still primarily a developer-led exercise. Integration is tricky, expensive, and prone to change. Tomorrow's AI software, however, will be more readily accessible and inclusive without significant development effort, meaning even small outfits and organizations can easily embed AI into their applications. It is true democratization of digital intelligence.

The result is a level of pervasiveness that is hard to fathom in today's world. AI will be as common as computers and smartphones are today. In fact, it will become so integrated and part of everything we do that it will be hard to clearly point to and say, "Aha! Now *that's* AI."

This will lead to a proliferation in the types of tasks AI can handle because it will be increasingly easy to add that feature to a variety of common tasks, needs, and applications. We're just at the beginning of this hockey stick curve of adoption. Hold onto your hats, we're not in Kansas anymore.

BLENDING OF PHYSICAL AND VIRTUAL

AI won't just be everywhere. It will be in everything. I have grown up in a world where most of my life has been spent in the virtual world. Software and code, data and databases, user interfaces and input devices. I lived in the physical world, but my mind was in this other, ethereal plane.

Things are quickly changing as technology becomes cheaper and more pervasive, and the cloud centralizes complex computing so that tiny "smart devices" can tap into the power of a mainframe. The result is the mega-trend "Internet of

Things" (IoT), which brings connectivity and intelligent automation to everything from refrigerators to stoplights.

Dave Copps, a Dallas-based three times successful entrepreneur (the proverbial Silicon Valley hat trick), has ridden the wave of AI expansion. In the past twenty years, he has founded three companies focused on artificial intelligence and machine learning. His most recent, Hypergiant Sensory Sciences, aims to transform in real time what's being captured by cameras in 2D into 3D models for spatial analytics.

The product's user interface looks more like a first-person-shooter video game than a traditional analytics tool. Clients can teleport and fly in and out of the models as they analyze what's going on. Projects in development range from search-and-rescue operations to remote sensing of large facilities.

"We give our clients superpowers in their ability to perceive and predict what's happening in their physical environments. Imagine being able to perceive and learn from all of your locations simultaneously."

MORE GENERALIZABLE AI

I don't see us realistically hitting the singularity anytime soon, where AI will become self-aware and create a virtuous (or vicious) cycle of ever-expanding capabilities. Our understanding of the mind and technology still has a long way to go before we achieve true Universal AI.

But AI is clearly a spectrum, and in the coming years, we will see a new class of tools and algorithms that are capable of learning a much broader set of skills than today's fairly specialized ones. The evolution will again lead to the pervasiveness of AI adoption as these tools become easier and quicker to train and move into service.

The dirty secret of today's AI is it requires an exorbitant amount of human intervention and coaching to get machines to a point where they are useful in even the most basic everyday tasks. The use case still needs to be pronounced enough to warrant the investment in human capital, even if the technical implementation is easier.

In the coming years, we will see improvements in self-tuning algorithms and tools that train other algorithms. "Machines making machines. Hmm. How perverse," as C-3PO says. These exist today and are getting increasingly better. Recent progress is especially promising.

IT'S ALL ABOUT YOU (NO, REALLY)

Let's get real for a moment. One of my AI pet peeves is how software often doesn't use what it knows about you. You're a software developer in Minnesota, yet your job searches continually list sales roles in Florida. You're a vegetarian, and your reservations app continually recommends steak houses. Privacy concerns being real and what they are, software can still help connect the dots without overstepping ethical bounds.

I had a software executive once share that they captured context about users but threw it out because "the search algorithm can do a better job of guessing what the user wants." Umm, what? He was convinced that based on a short, few-word query, a search engine could do better without including the context of whether it was a senior partner or associate, litigation or business attorney, a lawyer in Minnesota or California. Excuse me, sir, but I call bullsh**.

The reality is that much of this context can be gleaned from the environment and known information about knowledge workers without violating any concerns of privacy, real or perceived. In the near future, we will see an increase in this type of nuanced decision support, which will make the experience feel much more relevant and personalized.

When you tell Alexa to "reorder coffee," "she" knows what you last ordered and automatically pulls that into the shopping cart, even though Amazon has tens of thousands of options. When you tell Siri to "call back Jenn," "she" knows you mean your wife, even though you have lots of Jenns in your address book (like Matt, a pretty common name for a certain generation).

These examples are relatively constrained, but it shows the promise of what can be done with additional context. Increasingly, people will demand this improved performance, so long as the trade-off between privacy and efficiency is explicit and well understood.

FROM CONTENT CURATION TO CREATION

AI will be able to generate full-fledged and intelligible responses to a wide variety of topics, based on the large corpus of content both universally available as well as within your own history. As I said, personalized. Tools will be able to understand how you've responded to others in the past, even at the nuance of audience, and craft an appropriate reply.

Replying to an external client executive you haven't met before? Suit up and put on your best, well-articulated, intelligent response. Chatting with a colleague you've been together with for twenty years? Let the emojis fly. Audience is key, and AI tools will begin to understand those nuances.

The techniques for replying to conversations extend to social media and even free-form blog posts. Tools will be able to take a nugget of an idea from you, conduct research, and build an entire convincing narrative around it, all while using your prior posts to capture your tone and style. It's like having your own personal army of ghostwriters.

ORGANIZING YOUR DAY

We covered some of the heavy-hitting admin tasks and how those have been largely automated. In the near future, we will see a broadening of that automation to include all sorts of traditionally human-managed items, everything from expense reports and receipt management to proofreading not just for grammar but content, fact-checking, and style fitted to the audience.

New tools will be able to stitch data across internal and external systems more easily, synthesize that into a more tailored experience, and leverage more generalizable algorithms to learn your idiosyncrasies quickly. Combined, these improvements will lead to an immersive support experience—whether through tools like Alexa and Siri or in a yet-to-be-seen ethereal form.

Then, there's the world of resource and project management. That's right. Synergy, baby. As we talk about the nodes of our human cloud—freelance and gig work, even good old-fashioned contractors—the task of staffing projects with the right people and keeping everything on task is still a necessarily manual process. It is complicated, nuanced, and the wrong call can lead to tens or hundreds of thousands of dollars in lost opportunity.

But as with all areas, AI will continue to creep into the space of managing projects, first through custom-built tools tailored for this use case, then ultimately in commercial software like JIRA, Trello, Microsoft Project, ServiceNow, HR and recruiting systems like Workday and Taleo, and more. The reality is that much of the PM's and staffer's role is routine and low-value. Task-tracking, communication, agreements, and the like are all better handled by machines, leaving the high-value work of relationship, stakeholder, organizational change, and risk management to the human in the equation. As with other areas, we're talking augmentation, not replacement.

AI FOR AI

Ah, the delicious irony. Developers making themselves obsolete. Well, not exactly. But we are seeing a trend toward higher-order creation of websites, logos, software, and more. Early forays into this space are still rudimentary, but a lot of hype and investment is going into companies looking to drive innovation here. As AI becomes more robust, it is not hard to imagine many of the low-level tasks of designers and developers being relegated to software.

AI is a natural evolution, one that these creative technical types have always embraced. From the days of C++ to higher-level languages and development environments like Java and .NET, from early attempts to Adobe's and Apple's increasingly robust creative suites, the goal is simple: give developers tools that simplify the tedious and painful parts of their job so that they can focus on the architecture and creative aspects of their roles.

I was a lazy software developer, and the old maxim holds true. If you do something boring often enough, you automate it. That used to involve individual developers writing scripts to accomplish a task. Increasingly, this is software embedding AI to accomplish routine tasks for all developers. Ah, altruism meets laziness.

FINAL THOUGHTS

Take this entire chapter with a grain of salt. Predicting the future is both a fun and fraught process. Fun in that nothing can be proven upon the publishing of this book, and fraught in that ultimately everything will be under scrutiny as this book attempts to stand the test of time. Ah, the writer's dilemma.

For my part, I feel confident that these types of tasks will ultimately be available to you through AI-powered software, in a time horizon not far off from the decade after this book's release. But specific offerings, tools, and timing will certainly be subject to change and likely off, sometimes too soon, sometimes longer than anticipated, and from companies and tools not even envisioned yet.

The trends, however, are clear and unstoppable. Many of these capabilities are available in a limited capacity today. What we see in tomorrow's automated tasks is an improvement in quality and reliability, which only comes with time, effort, and investment.

CHEAT SHEET

Lesson 1: The machine cloud will become increasingly pervasive in everyday life, integrate more into our physical world, and be more applicable to our personal situation.

Lesson 2: While not quite achieving true human-level general intelligence anytime soon, AI will become more flexible and generalizable, which will further improve its general utility and costs to implement.

Lesson 3: We will increasingly need to embrace what is uniquely human about us and use our expert intelligence to orchestrate an army of intelligent systems.

WE DARE YOU

Activity 1: Think about your particular discipline, company, and industry. What will it look like in five years? Ten years? How will advanced technology like AI, virtual reality, and drones/sensors change it for the better? For the worse?

Activity 2: Pick one trend from your list above and set up an alert using your favorite web research system like Google or news. Have it send you new information about this topic at least once a month to stay current.

Activity 3: Read more about the future of the machine cloud.

BOOKS WE RECOMMEND

The Lights in the Tunnel: Automation, Accelerating Technology and the Economy of the Future by Martin Ford

The Singularity Is Near: When Humans Transcend Biology by Ray Kurzweil

HELLO, "NEW" WORLD!

16

RELEASE THE CHANGEMAKER

THE TIME IS NOW, THE CHANGEMAKER IS *YOU*; EMBRACE YOUR NEW MINDSET TO UNLOCK YOUR VITRUVIAN IDEAL

Dear You,

Yeah you. Ready to take on the world? Of course you are. If you need some help, we have expert designers, developers, writers, SEO experts, and even "customer experience ninjas" waiting for you in the human cloud. If you need more time, the machine cloud is ready to automate everything it can. For calendaring, we have Calendly. For editing, we have Grammarly. If you really want to get crazy, automate entire functions—your supply chain, your inbound sales channel. Do it right, and what once took a hundred people can happen through just you. And if you need control—control to work where you want, when you want, and on what you want—we have you covered. You can be a full-time freelancer. Or a full-time employee. Or somewhere in between. It doesn't matter how you embrace us, we got your back. We support you, the changemaker, through autonomy, flexibility, and resources once reserved only for large companies. And we can't wait to see the change you'll create in the world!

Sincerely,

The Human and Machine Clouds

How about we replace that initial social contract with the above? Sounds a hell of a lot better.

Sharon, the bookkeeper out of Boston, replaced a tyrannical boss with thirty-six clients, bringing in $26,000 a month and working on her own time. Lisa replaced a single job title and a couple of bullet points of responsibilities with the ability to do everything she wanted. For you, the human cloud unlocks a virtuous cycle of value. As Lisa put it, "The more you say yes, the more you can tap into your network and add value for yourself, the client, and the expert you connected with."

But we've intentionally kept one final secret from you—you need a new mindset to make the human and machine clouds worth it.

THE NEW YOU

Want to see what you will look like to mere mortals?

Pretty cool, huh?

Technically that's not you. It's the Vitruvian Ideal—the embodiment of the best version of us, the true Renaissance Person (with a hipster twist). And who's more

Renaissance than Leonardo da Vinci, the artist of this concept? We owe the world we live in today to da Vinci. He invented or dreamed of so much around us. He invented early flying and diving contraptions. He invented weapons. He even invented early robots! But, best of all, he embodies the best version of us we can all become.

By embracing the human and machine clouds, we can all be da Vinci. We can actually go one step further. We can invent, create, then scale our impact. Boy, would da Vinci be jealous.

But before we create the next *Mona Lisa*, we must build one last muscle. This muscle is the mindset that makes the human and machine clouds actionable. Remember, these new clouds are just a means, not an end. The end is the actual impact we have, and while the human and machine clouds are phenomenal tools to support us, without a mindset, we have no target to point to.

Most of us have been trained to have an obedience mindset. Listen, then memorize, whether that's orders from the teacher or the boss.

The changemaker mindset flips obedience on its head. As we learned earlier, we're the expert, and we work as self-organizing peers and collaborators. We, not the boss, dictate our own orders. And rather than memorizing, we align our energy with three priorities:

- Prioritize problems
- Prioritize experiences
- Prioritize relationships

Each priority is customizable. Your problems aren't the same as my problems. Your experience isn't my experience. But for both of us, if we integrate the changemaker mindset to applying the human and machine clouds, we will unlock our Vitruvian Ideal.

Prioritize Problems

It's no longer enough to be good. If it were, we'd still care about job titles. Instead, we need to be good at deeply understanding problems and being resourceful in how we solve them.

Take Melisha, a twenty-year-old computer science major at Kantipur Engineering College in Kathmandu, Nepal. Melisha isn't the typical computer scientist. She comes from a family of subsistence farmers in a rural village of Nepal. Her family did well. They raised more than forty cows, goats, and water buffaloes, and could even hire a small staff. But seven years ago, they faced an outbreak of anthrax that wiped out most of their herd—a devastating setback they are still struggling with today. This experience led Melisha to deeply care about livestock farming. She wanted to prevent an outbreak like that from ever happening again.

Melisha didn't seem all that different at first. She went to university to study computer science (work at a big tech company here we come). But instead of prioritizing the job search, she couldn't let go of that anthrax outbreak. While she had no relevant expertise in the traditional sense—she wasn't a farmer or a vet—she had a hunch that she could use what she was learning in computer science to help solve this problem. So, with the help of three classmates, she set out to solve this through the machine cloud.

Her team talked with farmers, researched livestock farming and veterinary practices, then built a monitoring device prototype that tracked the animals' temperatures, sleep patterns, stress levels, motion, and activities.

While the project is in its infancy, the results are outstanding. They've already prevented one deadly outbreak by identifying a cow that was in the early stages of sickness, allowing the farmer to quarantine the animal quickly and prevent the disease from spreading. They hit 95 percent accuracy in predicting an animal's health in their initial tests. And in 2017, they were named regional finalists in Microsoft's Imagine Cup Competition. What Melisha did was incredible. She identified a massive problem and is creating a solution that's on track to help millions of small farmers in remote corners of the world live prosperously. And although she wasn't the career fair warrior, it's safe to say that she won't have a hard time getting hired now.

Melisha understood she didn't need a job title. Or a logo on her resume. Instead, she needed a problem she could intensely care about and then solve it by embracing the machine cloud.

Your impact will be driven by problems, not job titles. I know, college didn't tell us to fall in love with problems. But our new resume in the human cloud does. It quantifies our impact according to whatever problem we align with.

Sharon's clients need accurate bookkeeping and financial forecasting. J's clients need to communicate a message through presentation design. Laszlo's customers need to be productive. Each of these superheroes focused on their particular problem and used the human and machine clouds as tools to solve for it.

How about you? Use your curiosity to identify your unique problem, then use the vision pyramid to align every single ounce of energy from here on out to that one problem.

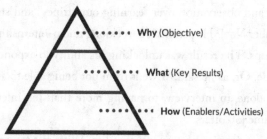

In understanding your *why*, what do you think about when you doze off? What do you find yourself doing when you're not "assigned" to something? Your why should seldom change. It's your North Star, the purpose of your professional life. Matt C's why is improving people's lives through artificial intelligence. Matt M's why is making the human cloud work for everyone. What's yours?

In the middle is your *what*, the strategy, and key results needed to achieve your *why*. This is fairly malleable. It may well change year to year as you evolve.

The bottom contains your actions. Read every night. Write from 4:00 to 8:00 (a.m. or p.m.). Your daily routine. This changes fairly often as you continuously improve.

Remember, your journey isn't a bunch of "set it and forget it" moments. It's the accumulation of experiences that build on top of each other in the same direction, en route to one aligned goal. This concept isn't new. What is new is the digitization of these experiences and the resulting speed by which you become hyper-relevant for the problem you align your effort with.

Prioritize Experiences

It's also no longer enough to pick one path and go through the motions.

By traditional terms, we'll all have multiple "careers." They won't look like careers. They'll look more like projects and experiments. And with these projects, we can't just punch in, crunch materials or numbers, then punch out. In traditional corporate culture, the intended outcome or success criteria of our effort is pleasing a boss. In today's world, the intended outcome of our effort is the resulting impact of what we create.

This shifts our mindset from obedient lapdogs to problem solvers prioritizing experimentation and observation over "earning our stripes" and staying within our lane. Remember Noel? He prioritized weeklong micro-internships over yearly summer internships. The result was unlocking his ability to exponentially prove effort and attitude. Or, as he said, "I went from not being able to attain a single opportunity, let alone an interview, to having more than ten interviews and a handful of full-time job offers."

Prioritizing experiences changed my own life. With just ten months of *real work experience*, I had the opportunity to build and lead a signature product at one of the most valuable tech companies in the world. Which, to be honest, I'm still baffled, shocked, and beyond grateful for because I didn't have to earn my stripes climbing the management chain to get this level of responsibility. Like Noel, instead of the traditional path of formal internships or entry-level roles, I focused on projects that required leading global and remote teams. Which meant I did in months what would have taken years via a traditional route. For example, one project implementing communication SOPs took under six months. Another validated a market opportunity and implemented the go-to-market strategy in under four months. The compounding result of these projects was that instead of a traditional resume saying I had ten months of real work experience, I came in with over five years of management experience, which gave me the street cred that led to the runway to build and lead a product at the age of twenty-six instead of waiting until I was thirty-six.

For Noel and myself, the result of prioritizing experiences was an increase in subsequent opportunities. The old "dog years" expression for accelerated growth used to apply to consulting and startups. Today, it applies to the human cloud since projects exponentially increase our opportunity feedback lens.

This shift in prioritization doesn't just accelerate subsequent opportunities. It also unlocks the autonomy and flexibility to control how we work. For Gordon Shotwell, our philosopher turned law student turned data scientist, focusing on adding a human touch to algorithms empowered him to ditch the safe but often miserable life of a corporate lawyer. According to Gordon, focusing on experiences over that linear ladder unlocked an exhilarating and flexible work environment. Same with J Cheema, chief of staff to a leadership team of twenty-six vice presidents at Nike. By prioritizing projects building executive presentations, J unlocked complete control of his life while earning over $350,000. As he told us, "I decide on my clients and projects and choose when and where to work. I'm in complete control of my day."

Prioritize Relationships

The days of the lone cowboy or mad scientist are at an end (if they ever existed to begin with). To succeed, we also need an intense focus on relationships to overcome our individual biological limitations. We need our own tribe.

The benefit of working within a company is that all resources are in one place—including all our work relationships. Whether it's the marketing lead helping you draft copy, the developer building your landing page, or the boss angling to steal your work, at least we have a sense of belonging that nurtures our social needs.

The human and machine clouds risk taking this away. Instead of being colocated in one place, resources are distributed globally on one network, with no one "assigned" but rather deciding to work with you.

On the surface, this can seem scary and shallow. How will I grow a relationship with no watercooler, no cafeteria, not even an office party? Yet for those who have worked in this world, you know the connections formed can be deeper than the office. Need proof? Here's me cooking with a freelancer in my tribe.

I know where her kids are going to college. Where they want to work after college. Honestly, most people mistake my relationship with my freelancers for family.

From left: Samantha Mason, Matthew Mottola

Let's face it—there is no escaping our universal human need to be productive and belong. We are social creatures, even us introverts and malcontents. We thrive on connection and utility, and while our work tribe, that group of people we used to associate closely with when we worked side by side from nine to five, may be disintegrating, it is being replaced with something even stronger: our life tribe.

In a tribe, whether it's our modern-day digital one or a small village in prehistoric Asia, fitting in is an evolutionary mandate. People strive, often at great cost, to be liked and needed. Being outcast from a tribe can be a fate worse than death.

But unlike those ancient days, when your tribe was the only game in town, in today's world the tables have turned. Individuals hold the power. Why? Because our tribe is what we make of it. Cliques be damned. If we don't like who we're playing with, we just pick up our toys and go find one of the literally billions of people on the internet who would be more than willing to play with us.

This shift in the power dynamic is at the core of the human cloud. It's not just about the reduction in friction that makes it possible, it's about the shift of power from a command-and-control corporation to individual choice. I get goose bumps just thinking about that level of empowerment.

For all of us who have been screwed over by a draconian boss, we're at that point in our story where the bad guy gets his comeuppance. In this new world, you steal someone's sh** and claim it as your own, and your tribe turns on you in a heartbeat.

You cannot hide. There's no team to do all your homework and projects for you. For some, that's exhilarating, for others it's terrifying. For those who build strong networks, deliver consistently superior work, and have a genuine desire to help and build deep relationships, the world is their horseradish-covered oyster. We are the new changemakers. And we are at the center of a vast network of resources, a constellation, just waiting for us to reach up into the stars and set our own fate.

RELEASE THE CHANGEMAKER

We started this book by telling you there's a gold rush of opportunity. That, instead of shovels, we have the human and machine clouds. That, instead of miners, we have you—the changemaker—to reject the status quo and change the world through 10x outcomes.

Well, now is your time.

What will you create? What will you change? The world *cannot* wait to see!

CHEAT SHEET

Lesson 1: We will unlock our own Vitruvian Ideal—the embodiment of the new Renaissance Person and a supercharged changemaker—by applying the human and machine clouds to a mindset that prioritizes problems, experiences, and relationships.

- **Prioritize Problems:** Since technology is moving too fast for traditional paths, we need to shift from caring about job titles to deeply understanding problems and being resourceful in how we solve them.

- **Prioritize Experiences:** Since we will have multiple careers that look more like projects, we need to shift from pleasing a boss, earning our stripes, and staying within our lane, to favoring experimentation and observation.

- **Prioritize Relationships:** Since talent is now distributed globally on one network, with no one assigned but rather deciding to work with you, creating outcomes at scale will be the result of the deep relationships within your tribe.

WE DARE YOU

Activity 1: Release your inner changemaker, and do more than we can ever dream of.

ACKNOWLEDGMENTS

To say that writing a book (like raising a child) takes a village would be an understatement. We literally wouldn't be here, talking with you, if it weren't for a few key people and a host of others entering our lives at serendipitous moments.

First and foremost is our agent, John Willig of Literary Services, Inc., who took a chance on two first-time authors and saw something great in the kernel that led to this book. John was instrumental in positioning the work and coaching us along the way. As we said before, thank goodness for the human cloud to help us find such a consummate expert and a bang-up good guy. Thanks, John!

Similarly, we wouldn't be here if not for Sara Kendrick, Senior Acquisitions Editor at HarperCollins Leadership. She "got" our message quickly and became a passionate advocate, getting the rest of the team over the line and leading to us being signed. Thanks for all of your efforts to let our voice and message be heard.

Finally, we would likely still be writing the first, mediocre draft if it were not for the amazing project management and editing skills of Samantha (Sam) Mason. She was part of the team from day one—another amazing human cloud find—and an integral part of making this project a success. And we'd like to think we made a great friend in the process.

FROM MATTHEW MOTTOLA

First and foremost, a huge thank-you to my coauthor, Matt Coatney. You have been nothing short of incredible throughout this journey. From balancing pancakes and stand-up calls, to dealing with my need for a mock wedding shoot, your dedication and passion for helping our readers is contagious. I expected awesome work from you, but I didn't expect to make a best friend. Thank you for making work seem more fun than a little kid's slumber party.

To my hometown of Newburyport, Massachusetts, I owe you everything. Specifically, the people who made it so special. Mentors Ken Jackman, Mike Trotta, and Gina Adamo, you've given me clarity and confidence every step of this journey. To my grandparents—you taught me to seek passion and help others in everything I do. To my aunt—you inspired me to teach. To my family and parents. And to the Keenes—thank you for the hotel (basically a bed-and-breakfast), the driving range in your backyard, and your support. To my teachers in Newburyport, specifically Mr. Sheridan, Mr. LaChapelle—never a stranger. And Mr. Dollas, my seventh- and eighth-grade English teacher, you instilled my love for the written word. In the words of my favorite country song—"This one's for my people back home."

Babson College, you taught me how to fall in love with problems and gave me the platform to be an entrepreneur. Specifically, Dean Rollag for teaching me how to lead, Professor Goulding for teaching me how to dissect problems logically, and Professor Reza for instilling a love for travel and Asia.

In my working career, I've been fortunate to work with incredible teams, organizations, and the individuals in this book. Entrepreneur First, specifically Shiu Lun Tsang, Bernadette Cho, Jess Chang, Didier Vermeiren, and Teik Guan Tan, you took a way-too-confident entrepreneur and gave me the stage to actually build this future of work. You've been incredible mentors, advisors, and one hell of a force for growth. Dan Sheehan, thanks for protecting us from the antithesis of this book. Arn Rubinoff at Georgia Tech, thank you for being a role model, mentor, and giving me a shot in higher education. Gigster, you showed me what's possible with the human cloud. John Burrell, thank you for the runway to be an entrepreneur within Gigster. Chris Tosswill, thank you for being a mentor and champion in helping me create ideation. Brandon Bright, Ryan Borker, and Sandrine Bitton, you're three of the most knowledgeable people at driving outcomes in the human cloud. Thank you to the team at Microsoft and Upwork that made the Microsoft 365 freelance toolkit happen, specifically Jackie Pak, Don Forrest (always best-dressed), Eric Gilpin, Marc Hosein, and Kate Adams. And to the best boss I've ever had—Liane Scult—you've been a role model, leader, changemaker, and friend. You taught me how to be the boss I hope to become.

FROM MATTHEW COATNEY

My most sincere thanks first go to Matt Mottola, without whom I would not be part of the book. He saw early on a need for a technical coauthor with a deep background in artificial intelligence, and thankfully through another human cloud moment, I had just written some smaller technical pieces with him. What he didn't know he would get is an enigma of a middle-aged executive with a rebellious and creative streak, as well as a would-be English professor ("Do we use a hyphen? An en dash? An em dash?").

Family most always gets an appreciative nod in the acknowledgments, and this is no exception. My wife, Jenn, and my kids, Parker, Chase, and Lacey, have remained supportive of all of my "side passion projects," of which this is one of the few that panned out. Jenn keeps my head at least tethered close to the ground so that my dreams have a chance to sprout legs.

I cannot begin to thank my parents, Doug and Jane, enough. My dad passed on his kind, selfless attitude (which I aspire to daily even when I don't achieve), and my mom passed on an insatiable thirst for knowledge and lifelong learning. Through that combination of genes, I also got my technical streak, as many of my cousins, uncles, and grandfathers are well-reputed scientists and engineers.

Thanks go to my master's program and thesis advisor, Srinivasan Parthasarathy of The Ohio State University, and my first tech startup experience, Leadscope. I stumbled into both as I was trying to figure out what I wanted to be when I grew up, and it was the perfect one-two punch of theoretical and applied artificial intelligence that jump-started my career.

Throughout my working career, so many people have influenced me in one way or another, far too many to thank individually. But you know who you are. I do want to call special attention to two people who have been longtime mentors, staying in touch across jobs and states: Andy Morris and Mike Sweeney. Thank you both for your continued support, listening, and advice.

A special note of thanks also goes to Katrina Kittle, my high school home-room advisor and English teacher. She inspired me to write, and I told her one day I would be an author. Well, this isn't the next great American novel, but I'll take it all the same.

ACKNOWLEDGMENTS

TO OUR HUMAN CLOUD COLLABORATORS

And last, from both of us, thanks to the digital collaborators who made this book possible, For those reading this, below are some of the best and brightest changemakers in the human cloud.

- Lauren Detweiler, marketing expert who created the go-to-market plan and opportunity analysis.
- Emerson Mendieta-Castro, designer who led creating the print visuals, along with the presentations and web pages that led to this book.
- Erica Ciko Campbell, writer who mastered how we connected and presented the Vitruvian Ideal.
- Seth Brown, writer who added comedic gold to scripts and presentations leading to this book.
- J Cheema, designer who created the keynote presentations that led to this book.
- Dave Copps, entrepreneur who shared his story of creating companies that bring AI to a broader audience.
- David Guggenheim, media expert who helped shape our go-to-market plan.
- Jacqueline Liu, writer who created the cheat sheets for each chapter.
- Careen Maloney, journalist and writer who led creating each story.
- Adam Marinelli, LinkedIn profile expert who helped shape the understanding of how to position one's digital profile.
- Brad Miller, writer who contributed examples of the machine cloud.
- Simon Rhee, speechwriter who shaped the scripts and presentations leading to this book.
- Ahmed Zaeem, designer who created visuals for the book.
- Scott D. S. Young, designer who created visuals for this book.
- Joseph Kelly, research analyst and editor who beta tested our full manuscript.
- Sally Shupe, editor who beta tested our full manuscript.
- Nicole d'Entremont, editor who beta tested our full manuscript.

- Elaine Pofeldt, journalist and expert on the landscape and the mechanics behind one-person businesses.
- Chad Nesland, procurement executive who advised our understanding of how enterprises scale the freelance economy.
- Siddharth Suri, researcher and author who advised our understanding of the human cloud's implications in training artificial intelligence algorithms.
- Devin Fidler, founder who helped us understand the implications of automation of the human cloud on management.
- Matthew May, innovation executive and expert who provided feedback and helped us navigate the publishing landscape.
- Brandon Bright, software consultant who shared his story of helping a Fortune 500 organization embrace the human cloud.
- Noel Arrellano, student who shared his story of unlocking access to relevant experience via freelance projects through Parker Dewey.
- Sharon Heath, freelance expert who shared her story of growing her accounting practice in the human cloud.
- Cat Casey, executive who shared her story of bridging technologists and lawyers.
- Gordon Shotwell, who shared his story of both working in the human cloud and helping to make AI more understandable to non-technologists.
- Tony Trippe, an entrepreneur using the machine cloud to help other inventors.
- David Vishanoff, a professor and researcher who uses the machine cloud to help improve our understanding of cultures and religions.
- Vin Vomero, an entrepreneur who shared his amazing story of using AI to make assessing properties better.
- Dave White, a freelance expert and artist who shared his amazing story of combining accounting with his love for art.

Thanks to all of you for making this book something more than some bound pages on a physical or digital shelf.

The Matthews

INDEX

A

abuse, 5
Accenture, 93
Adecco, 93
Adidas, xi, 50
Airbnb, 122
Air Pods, 141
Alexa, 147
Alike (film), ix
Amazon, 45, 46, 160
Amazon AWS, 95, 96, 142
Amazon Web Services (AWS), 9
American Dream, 44–45
American Express, 142
amplification effect, 23
analytical skills, importance of, 132–33
Anheuser-Busch, 43
Apple Mail, 140
Application Programming Interfaces
    (APIs), 143
Arellano, Noel, 43–46
Arruda, Andrew, 17, 118
artificial intelligence (AI)
    analytical skills needed to work with,
        132–33
    expert intelligence vs., 123
    freelancers, AI, 136–50
    future of, 158–66
    and knowledge workers, 119
    for large businesses, 154
    logic/reasoning skills needed to work
        with, 132
    managing, 128
    opportunity afforded by, 123–24
    organizational skills needs to work with,
        131

    predictive power of, 133
    and situational leadership, 128–30
    for small businesses, 152
Asana, 15
AT&T, 25
augmentation potential, human cloud,
    80–81
automation
    identifying targets for, 137–39
    increasing, 119–20
aviation, 122–23

B

Bain Capital, 93
Bank of America, 142
Bing, 143
Bloomberg, 16
Blue Nile, 50
Bluetooth, 95
Boeing, 16
Boston Consulting Group, 93
Boston University, 47
Box, 15
brainstorming, 138
Bright, Brandon, xi, 39, 93, 94, 97
Brown, Brené, 24
Brynjolfsson, Erik, 27
bullies, 10

C

caffeine, 148
calendars, managing, 139–40
Calendly, 66, 139
Caloriemamma.ai, 148
Campbell, Bill, 4, 107
Campbell, Erica Ciko, 45

car, buying a, 20

career growth, 110

careers, 174

Casey, Cat, 17, 126–27, 131

changemaker(s), x–xi

  challenge of being a, 23–24

  the cloud and potential power of,
    24–25

  difficulty of retaining, 4

  releasing your inner, 169–78

  rise of the, 20–22

change orders, 66, 87

chatbots, 141–42, 152

Cheat Sheet(s)

  for applying your skills to the machine
    cloud, 134–35

  for augmenting yourself via the human
    cloud, 78–79

  for becoming a human-cloud freelancer,
    67–68

  for embracing the human cloud, 98–99,
    106

  for future human-cloud trends, 112–13

  for future machine-cloud trends,
    165–66

  for hiring freelancers via the human
    cloud, 90–91

  for imagining yourself as a changemaker,
    26–27

  for leveraging AI to your organization's
    advantage, 156–57

  for leveraging the machine cloud to your
    advantage, 149–50

  for moving to the human cloud, 54–56

  for releasing your inner changemaker,
    177–78

  for understanding the broken office,
    11–12

  for understanding the machine cloud,
    124–25

  for understanding the rise of the human
    cloud, 39–40

Cheema, J, x–xi, 18, 49–50, 52, 53, 77,
  175

Chemical Abstracts, 143

Chesterton, Scott, 157

Choudary, Sangeet Paul, 40

Christian, Brian, 125

A Christmas Story (film), 10

Cisco Talent Cloud, 103

CliffsNotes, 145

the cloud, 9

  perils of, 22–23

  and potential power of changemakers,
    24–25

  your relationship with the, 17–20

  see also human cloud; machine cloud

Coda, 147

collaborators, network of, 76

Colvin, Geoff, 27

communication

  expectations about, 65–66

  for onboarding, 87

  with virtual teams, 89

complex tasks, managing, 147

connectivity, improved, 118–19

consulting agencies, 34, 93

contained tasks, 138

contingencies

  expectations about, 66

  and onboarding, 87

Copps, Dave, 161

credit, others taking, 4–6

CS DISCO, 126

C-suite, 8

cultural issues, 102

customizability, 25

D

Dare to Lead (Brown), 24

da Vinci, Leonardo, 45, 171

decision support tools, 122, 159–60

Deloitte, 93

dictation tools, 141

differentiators, 130

Doerr, John, 91

Doodle, 139

Do/Teach/Learn continuum, 62

download speeds, 119
Dropbox, 15, 152, 153

E
Eagle, Alan, 91, 113
eBay, 96
Einstein, 152
Elance, 34
Elsevier, 143
emails, responding to, 6, 140–42
employee(s)
  challenges managing, 127–28
  creating incentives for, to tap into the
    human cloud, 102–3
  empowering, 97–98
  legal classification of, 101–2
  problems with today's workplace from
    perspective of, 5–7
  shift to freelancers from, 36
empowerment, employee, 97–98
Entrepreneur, 112
Etsy, 58
European Union (EU), 102
Exaptive, 144
"Excel skills," 133
executives, working with, 42
expectations
  aligning your, 65–66
  and onboarding, 87
experiences, prioritizing, 173–75
expert intelligence, 123
ExxonMobil, xi, 50

F
feedback
  expectations about, 66
  getting, 44
  and onboarding, 87
Fidler, Devin, 108
"Fifty Shades of Blockbuster," 95–97
Fiverr, 96
flagging messages, 140
Ford, Henry, 75
Ford, Martin, 166

Foxy AI, 146–47
Freelancer.com, 34
freelancer(s)
  AI, 136–50
  becoming a human-cloud, 67–68
  finding opportunities as a, 63–64
  "handbooks" for, 87
  hiring, via the human cloud, 86,
    90–91
  legal classification of, 101–2
  machine cloud for, 152
  moving to full-time work from, 50–52
  origin of term, 34
  reasons to work as a, 59
  working like a, 16
fu**ckups, 66, 87
future trends
  with human cloud, 107–13
  with machine cloud, 158–66
The Future Workplace Experience (Meister
  and Mulcahy), 103

G
GCP, 94
GE, xi, 25, 50
General Data Protection Regulation
  (GDPR), 102
Georgia Tech, 77
Gigster, 94, 95
Gmail, 118, 141
GMass, 17, 118, 141
goals, defining the requirements for your,
  81–85
Goel, Ajay, 17, 21, 118, 141
Gold Star Bookkeeping, 35
Google, 140, 143, 147, 160
Google Chrome, 145
Google Cloud, 142
Google Docs, 88
Google Drive, 15
Google Flights, 142
Google searches, 18, 63–64, 74
Grove, Andy, 82
G Suite, 14, 15, 34, 42, 103

H

"handbooks," freelancer, 87
Harvard Business Review, 108
healthy, staying, 147–49
Heath, Sharon, 32–36, 58
Heimans, Jeremy, 27
Hersey, Paul, 135
Hinsenn, Peter, 4
hiring, via the human cloud, 86, 90–91
Hollywood model, 94
Hopper, 142
house2vec, 146
How (in Vision Pyramid), 62, 68
human cloud, 14–17, 31–113
  and accessing others' skills and talents, 72–73
  and advantage of small size, 95–97
  aligning your expectations from the, 65–66
  and becoming hyper-relevant, 59–62
  building long-term relationships via the, 66–67, 76–77
  building on current utilization of, 105
  building organizations around, 38–39
  creating a new resume for the, 45–46
  creating incentives for employees to tap into the, 102–3
  cultural issues of working with the, 102
  and death of the American Dream, 44–45
  and defining the requirements for your goal, 81–85
  discovering the potential of freelancing via the, 63–64
  and distribution of opportunity, 94–95
  embracing the, 92–106
  and employee empowerment, 97–98
  exponential scaling using the, 74–75
  and facilitating career growth, 110
  future trends with, 107–13
  hiring freelancers via the, 86
  and identity management, 109–10
  improving management via the, 107–8

  and in-product experience, 112
  jumping into the, 52–53
  knowing what you want from the, 58–59
  legal issues of working with the, 101–2
  machine cloud vs., 17
  managing teams via the, 87–89
  and maximizing enterprise spend, 110–11
  and moving from freelancer to corporate, 50–52
  as new opportunity, 34–35
  and non-traditional work, 47–49
  onboarding via the, 86–87
  organizing the, 111–12
  physical office vs., 15
  and "portability of merit," 108–9
  and productivity tools, 103
  reasons for moving to the, 41–56
  rise of the, 31–40
  setting up a program for working with the, 104–5
  and startups, 95–98
  tapping into the, 69–91
  and thinking like a network, 70–72
  thriving in the, 57–68
  as a tool, 35–36
  and using Google for expertise, 73–74
  working in the, 36–38
Hyman, Louis, 40
Hypergiant Sensory Sciences, 161
hyper-relevant, becoming, 59–62

I

IBM, 96, 160
IBM Watson, 17, 118, 142, 146
identifying the problem, 129
identity management, 109–10
IFTTT, 147
Imagine Cup Competition, 172
independent contractors, 101–2
individual, shift of power to the, 13–14
information, summarizing, 145–47

in-product experience, 112
Instagram, 25
Intel, 82
intellectual property (IP), 103
Internet of Things, 119, 160–61
internships, micro-, 44
Intuit, 4
InVision, 94

J
Jarvis, Paul, 79
Java, 94
Jia, Marlene, 157
JIRA, 15, 34, 89, 164
job titles, 172
Johns Hopkins University, 49
Johnson, Nicholas L., 40

K
The Karate Kid (film), 10
Kelly, Kevin, 12
Kessler, Sarah, 56
key performance indicators (KPIs), 95
King, Dave, 144
knowledge workers, 119
Kotlin, 94
Kurzweil, Ray, 166

L
large companies, machine cloud for,
    153–56
leadership
    servant, 4
    situational, 128–30
The Lean Startup (Ries), 72
learnable tasks, 138
Lee, Kai-Fu, 125
legal concerns, 101–2
LinkedIn, 50
Lisefski, Benek, 23, 64
logical skills, importance of, 131–32
long-term relationships, building, 66–67,
    76–77
Lucidchart, 153

M
Ma Bell, 111
machine cloud, 17, 117–66
    and advances in technology, 118–19
    analytical skills for dealing with the,
        132–33
    automation and impact of, 119–20
    and blending of the physical and the
        virtual, 160–61
    conducting research via the, 142–45
    and deciding what to automate,
        137–39
    defining the, 117
    and "everyday AI," 159–60
    and evolution of AI, 164
    future trends with, 158–66
    and generalizable AI, 161–62
    human cloud vs., 17
    and large companies, 153–56
    logic/reasoning skills for dealing with
        the, 131–32
    managing complex tasks using the,
        147
    managing teams via the, 127–28
    and managing travel, 142
    organizational skills for dealing with
        the, 130–31
    personalization of content with,
        162–63
    and responding to email, 140–42
    rise of the, 117–25
    and scheduling, 139–40, 163–64
    and shifting nature of work, 120–24
    and situational leadership, 128–30
    and small companies, 152
    summarizing information with the,
        145–47
    supercharging your organization with
        the, 151–57
    tapping into the, 136–50
    using AI freelancers from the,
        136–50
    working in the, 126–35
    see also artificial intelligence (AI)

Mailchimp, 143
manager(s)
  primary job of, 107
  problems with today's workplace from
    perspective of, 7–9
Manpower, 93
Mason, Samantha, 47–50, 176
master service agreements (MSAs), 87
McAfee, Andrew, 27
McKinsey, 93
meetings, 66–67
Meister, Jeanne C., 103, 106
Mendieta-Castro, Emerson, 73–74, 77
Mezi, 142
micro-internships, 44
Microsoft, 50, 89, 96, 101, 160, 172
Microsoft 365, 52, 110
Microsoft Azure, 142
Microsoft Forms, 52
Microsoft Office, 145, 152
Microsoft Outlook, 140
Microsoft Project, 164
Microsoft SharePoint, 143
Microsoft Teams, 15, 52, 89, 140
The Million-Dollar, One-Person Business
  (Pofeldt), 71, 152
Moazed, Alex, 40
moonlighting, 36
MRI scans, ix
Mulcahy, Kevin J., 103, 106
Musk, Elon, 61

N
Nadler, Laszlo, 74–75, 81
Nasdaq, 50
network
  of collaborators, 76
· thinking like a, 70–72
networks, 19
Neuralink, 61
New York Times, 143
nexxworks, 4
Nike, x, 18, 49, 175
99designs, 96

Node.js, 94
nodes, 19
nonprofit organizations, 152
Noom, 148
The Notebook (Sparks), 80
Nova Scotia, 131

O
obedience mindset, 171
oDesk, 34
Ogilvy, 70
OKR framework, 82–83
onboarding, 86–87, 103
Open Calais, 146
Oracle, 96
O'Reilly, Tim, 12
organizational skills, importance of,
  130–31
organization(s), 4
  AI-driven, 156
  building, around the human cloud,
    38–39
  supercharging your, 151–57
org charts, 71, 76

P
Pana, 142
Parker, Geoffrey G., 40
Parker Dewey platform, 43–44
Paro, 34, 58
Patinformatics, 143
"paying your dues," 6
Personally Identifiable Information (PII),
  102
physical offices, 15–16
Pink, Daniel, 20, 56
Pofeldt, Elaine, 71, 75, 79, 152
portable merit, 108–9
Power Automate, 52
PowerBI, 52
privacy issues, 102
problem(s)
  identifying the, 129
  prioritizing, 171–73

Procter & Gamble, 25
productivity tools, 103, 139–40, 153
projects, looking at work as, 16

Q
Questrom School of Business, 47
Qur'an, 144

R
racial bias, 24
Rally's Real Appeal, 148
Randstad, 93
Rate My Professors, 20–21
React, 94
reasoning skills, importance of, 131–32
relationships
    building long-term, 66–67, 76–77
    prioritizing, 175–77
reorganizations, 6, 7
repetitive tasks, 137
reply.ai, 142
research, conducting, 142–45
resume, creating a unique, 45–46
Rethinkery, 108
Revolution Growth, 50
Ries, Eric, 91
Rifkin, Jeremy, 12
Robert Half, 93
Robison, Peter, 16
Roboresponse, 142
robots, 121–22, 137
Rosenberg, Jonathan, 91, 113
Ross, Alex, 12
ROSS Intelligence, 17, 118, 120, 143

S
Salesforce, 152
scaling and scalability, 25, 74–75
scheduling, 139–40, 163–64
Schmidt, Eric, 91, 113
Scult, Liane, 50–52, 97
secretiveness, 6–7
self-doubt, 48
servant leadership, 4

ServiceNow, 164
sexism, 7
shadow IT, 153
SharePoint, 52
Shotwell, Gordon, xi, 17, 131–32, 175
Siegel, Eric, 150
Siemens, 50
Silicon Valley, 4, 61, 107
Silver, Nate, 135
singularity, 161
Siri, 147
situational leadership, and AI, 128–30
Sketch, 94
skills
    accessing others' talents and, 72–73,
        94–95
    analytical, 132–33
    "Excel," 133
    logic/reasoning, 131–32
    organizational, 130–31
Slack, 15, 34, 42, 89, 103, 140, 143, 153
small companies, machine cloud for, 152
small size, advantages of, 95–97
smartphones, 118
Smartsheet, 153
SMART tactics, 62
SMMRY, 145
"social contract," of today's workplace,
    3, 13
social networks, 19
social support, 23
software as a service (SaaS), 153
SolarCity, 61
Sparks, Nicholas, 80
specific, being, 62
staffing firms, 34
standard operating procedures (SOPs),
    42, 110
Stanford prison experiment, 8
startups, 95–98
statements of work (SOWs), 66, 84–87
success, traditional view of, 110
SurveyMonkey, 143
Swift, 94

T

Taleo, 164

teams, managing, 81, 87–89, 127–28

technology

cloud and shift in, 9–10

machine cloud and advances in, 118–19

see also artificial intelligence (AI)

temp agencies, 34

templates, 89

Tesla, 61

Texas A&M University, 43, 46

Thomson Reuters, 146

Thumbtack, 58

time management, 139–40, 163–64

Timms, Henry, 27

Tools4Wisdom, 75, 81

To Sell Is Human (Pink), 20

toxic cultures

from employee's perspective, 5–7

from manager's perspective, 7–9

traditional workplace

problems with, from employee's perspective, 5–7

problems with, from manager's perspective, 7–9

"social contract," of, 3

and technology shift, 9–10

training AI systems, 129–30

travel, managing, 142

Trello, 14, 15, 34, 42, 89, 103, 140, 164

tribes, creating, 175–77

Trippe, Tony, 143–44

TurboTax Live, 112

U

Uber, 122

UNC-Chapel Hill, 49

"Unified Field Theory," 61

Universal AI, 161

University of Oklahoma, 144

Upwork, x–xi, 14, 18, 34, 36–37, 45, 47, 49–50, 96

US Air Force, 124

Utrip, 142

V

Van Alstyne, Marshall W., 40

Vance, Ashlee, 61

Van Elegem, Laurence, 4

verbal abuse, 5

virtual teams, managing, 81, 87–89, 127–28

Vishanoff, David, 144–45

vision board, creating a, 68

Vision Pyramid, 61–62

visual property intelligence, 146

Vitruvian Ideal, 170–71

Vomero, Vin, 146–47

W

Wall Street Journal, 101

Walsh, Mike, 157

What (in Vision Pyramid), 62, 68

Wheelan, Charles, 135

White, Dave, 58–59

Why (in Vision Pyramid), 61–62, 68

Wordzen, 141

work, shifting nature of, 120–24

workbacks, 81–82

Workday, 164

X

X.ai, 139–40

Y

Yao, Mariya, 157

YouTube, xi, 31, 50, 72

Z

Zapier, 147

Zhou, Adelyn, 157

Zillow, 146–47

Zimbardo, Philip G., 8

Zoho, 143

ABOUT THE AUTHORS

Matthew Mottola builds the technology that brings the human cloud to market. He cofounded and is the CEO of Venture L—the operating system where today's top freelancers run their businesses. At Microsoft, he built the Microsoft 365 freelance toolkit, bringing Microsoft from a nascent to an industry leader. As a product leader, serial entrepreneur, and keynote speaker, his work has been broadly adopted by individuals, startups, SMBs, and Fortune 100s.

Matthew Coatney has twenty-five years of experience bringing AI and automation technologies to market in a variety of industries and for some of the largest global organizations. He has held a number of executive, product, and technology roles during his career and currently serves as CTO for a large consultancy and managed services provider. He is a frequent speaker and author on AI and the future of automation, including a TEDx Talk.